Give a Dock a Good Name?

By

Ken McCarron

Adrian Jarvis

First published 1992 by Merseyside Port Folios,
1 & 3 Grove Road, Rock Ferry,
Birkenhead, Wirral, Merseyside L42 3XS.

Merseyside Port Folios is the joint publishing imprint of the National
Museums and Galleries on Merseyside and Countyvise Limited.

Printed by Birkenhead Press Limited,
1 & 3 Grove Road, Rock Ferry,
Birkenhead, Wirral, Merseyside L42 3XS.

ISBN 0 9516129 4 8

NATIONAL MUSEUMS & GALLERIES
· ON MERSEYSIDE ·

Merseyside Port Folios

Merseyside Port Folios is a joint imprint of the Trustees of the National Museums and Galleries on Merseyside (NMGM) and Countyvise Ltd, set up to produce a series of occasional booklets on subjects in the history of Merseyside's Docklands.

The Merseyside Port Folios series began as a joint initiative between National Museums and Galleries on Merseyside and the Merseyside Development Corporation. The Museum seconded Adrian Jarvis, the Series Editor, to manage a small research team, and provided accommodation and all the usual office services, while the Development Corporation made a substantial financial contribution. That contribution allowed the employment of a Research Assistant, an Illustrator and a Data Clerk on short term contracts. A substantial book, together with the previous volumes in this series and a number of academic papers resulted, and it is hoped that these made some contribution to the understanding of the history of the Port of Liverpool.

Although that is all history now, most of the work that went into the preparation of this booklet was undertaken by Ken McCarron, the Research Assistant, and I record my thanks to him, as also to the Merseyside Development Corporation who made his involvement possible. As always, our colleagues in the Maritime Record Centre climbed innumerable stairs in finding and producing documents. Kate and Clare in our photography department respectively found and printed all the old negatives, and Colin Pitcher (freelance photographer) produced most of the new photographs.

In one sense, this Port Folio is completely different from the others in that the idea of producing it did not come from the Port Survey team. It came from Museum visitors, who pestered our 'front of house staff' with questions about how Salthouse/Dukes/Sandon etc Dock got its name. We are indebted to those who made the enquiries and to those who passed them on to me, because it is all too easy to research a subject and produce publications without ever quite understanding what it is that our customers really want to know.

Adrian Jarvis
Series Editor

Table of Contents.

Introduction

At the meeting of the Mersey Docks and Harbour Board on 18 May 1876, during a discussion on the naming of Langton Dock, T.B. Forwood was reported as saying "And was it not fitting that when strangers went over the roll call of the docks, and their education taught them without a guide that the Waterloo, the Wellington, the Trafalgar, the Nelson spoke of great battles and great heroes, of which we islanders were proud, so when a stranger asked who Langton was, his guide would tell him he was a Liverpool merchant, whose best years were spent in disinterested efforts to extend the fame of England's commerce, and who has contributed to make these docks of his native town the admiration of the world". How many people today know of Langton or indeed of many of the others after whom the Docks of the Mersey are named?

The question as to why Liverpool has docks and so many of them, is a very broad one and really outside the scope of this work. The interested reader is directed to the relevant part of the bibliography for greater detail. Put simply, the docks developed as a reaction to the tidal range of the Mersey. Some ports, for example Southampton, are able to do without enclosed wet docks, the change in tide being only a small vertical distance which means a ship tied up at a quay moves only a couple of metres up and down. On the Mersey, however, that movement at a quay open to the river can exceed ten metres. In the early days of the port, it was quite possible for a ship to rest on the mud at low water. But ships are designed to carry their load uniformly distributed over the whole of the immersed part of the hull, and the larger they get, the more difficult it is to design them so that they can stand on their bottoms without suffering damage. As ships got larger, therefore, it became necessary to provide docks in which they could remain afloat at all states of the tide. The only alternative was to anchor in the river and discharge into lighters, and here the fearful tidal rip of the Mersey came into play, making such procedures not merely costly, but difficult and dangerous. The first dock, soon to be known as the Old Dock, was begun in 1709 and many more were to follow.

The Corporation of Liverpool's Dock Committee and the Mersey Docks and Harbour Board/Company (MD&HB or MD&HC) at one time or another had around fifty docks under their control. The inexact nature of this figure is due to a looseness in the term 'dock' - does one include the three

Alexandra Branch Docks as separate docks or part of the whole? The figure of fifty counts all the individual names but in 1927 for the opening of Gladstone Dock the MD&HB claimed in different places within the same publicity material to have 87 and 90 docks - even they weren't sure! To this day, a signpost directing lorries from M57 and M58 to the docks reads "Docks 1-98". During construction a dock would be referred to as, for example, 'New North Dock' or, if a number of docks were being constructed concurrently, by letters (e.g. Dock 'H'). Names were normally assigned near to opening date and formalised in the official ceremony. The name of the dock or group of branch docks is what identified it as a separate unit for administrative and practical purposes, and it is the origin of these names that this book will trace. Most dock names fall into one of two broad groups, those named after people and those after places.

Docks which were named after people were either called after royalty or as political tributes to people who had helped Merseyside's trade in one way or another. The places either referred to the location of the dock, where the main trade carried on in the dock came from or went to, or commemorated famous military or naval victories. There are also a few anomalous names which fit into neither of these categories, deriving mainly from their function, such as the Union Dock or the Great Float.

Giving a dock a name was a way of honouring people, places or events and also served to avoid some of the potential for misunderstanding inherent in referring to docks by numbers or letters. However, when a new branch dock was built at Huskisson the following notice, issued on 30 December 1898 probably did little to eliminate possible confusion:

> "Notice is hereby given that it has been decided to change the names of the existing Branch Docks out of the Huskisson Dock forthwith as follows:-
>
> that now known as No. 2 will be known as No. 3
> that now known as No. 1 will be known as No. 2
>
> The new Branch Dock to be constructed immediately to the south of what will henceforth be No. 2 Branch Dock will be known as the Huskisson Branch Dock No. 1.
>
> By Order
> Miles Kirk Burton"

The number change was carried out to have the branch docks running 1, 2, 3 in order but the confusion over the first few days must have been significant. The old number two, now number three, was also the first one to be built. Other name changes only occurred after major redevelopments, though a few docks had alternative names proposed before they were opened. This booklet will discuss each dock that came under the auspices of the MD&HB and consider a small part of its history and the origin of its name.

A note on apostrophes.
It is quite common to find some dock names spelled with an apostrophe, as in George's Dock, Prince's Dock etc. The present writers have been unable to establish to their satisfaction which is correct, but there seems, just about, to be a majority in favour of no apostrophe in the numerous sources used, so apostrophes have been omitted throughout.

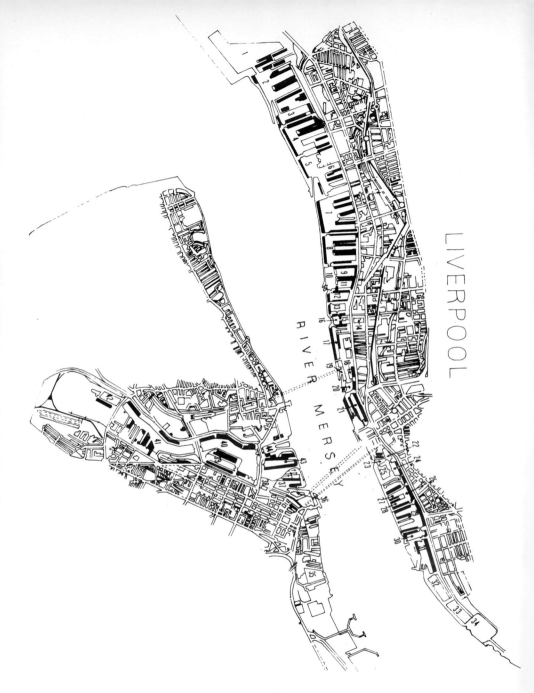

Liverpool and Birkenhead Docks 1991.

viii

KEY TO DOCK NAMES

1. Seaforth Container Terminal. Royal Seaforth Docks.
2. Gladstone Dock and Branch Docks Nos. 1 & 2.
3. Hornby Dock.
4. Alexandra Dock and Branch Docks Nos. 1, 2 & 3.
5. Langton Dock.
6. Brocklebank Dock and Branch Dock.
7. Canada Dock and Branch Docks Nos. 1, 2 & 3.
8. Huskisson Dock and Branch Docks Nos. 1, 2 & 3.
9. Sandon Dock.
10. Sandon Half-tide Dock.
11. Wellington Dock.
12. Bramley-Moore Dock.
13. Nelson Dock.
14. Stanley Dock.
15. Collingwood Dock.
16. Salisbury Dock.
17. Trafalgar Dock.
18. East Waterloo Dock.
19. West Waterloo Dock.
20. Princes half-tide Dock.
21. Princes Dock.
22. Canning Dock.
23. Canning Half-tide Dock.
24. Salthouse Dock.
25. Albert Dock.
26. Wapping Dock.
27. King's Dock No. 2.
28. King's Dock No. 1.
29. Queens Dock and Branch Docks No. 1 & 2.
30. Coburg Dock.
31. Brunswick Dock.
32. Toxteth Dock.
33. Harrington Dock.
34. Herculaneum Dock and 4 Graving Docks.
35. Cammell Lairds Fitting Out Basin
36. Morpeth Branch Dock.
37. Morpeth Dock.
38. Egerton Dock.
39. Vittoria Dock.
40. East Float
41. West Float.
42. Bidston Dock.
43. Wallasey Dock.
44. Alfred Dock.

Albert Dock

Commenced 1841 Opened 1845 Closed 1972

Albert Dock c. 1910. The vessel in the foreground is one of Harrisson's 'brandy boats' whose merchandise was bottled here.

Thanks to television and tourism, Albert is the best known of the Merseyside docks but it is at the same time the least typical of them all. What makes it so unusual and so attractive is the looming presence of the huge blocks of warehouses. Designed for the secure storage of goods, they were built after a period of fierce opposition from vested interests in the warehousing and carting trades. They were the first dockside warehouses in Liverpool readily available for public use. The warehouses were probably the first buildings in the world specifically designed for cargo handling by machines but they were actually built before the Armstrong hydraulic cranes were available for use. Despite this the Albert Dock itself was very much a white elephant. The dock was very quickly found to be too small and entrance to it was difficult. By 1890 it was underused and in 1899 one of the warehouse blocks - D block, now the Merseyside Maritime

Museum - was turned into a cold store. While the dock struggled, the Warehouses prospered, remaining much in demand for the storage and re-packaging of bonded goods until 1972 when the South Docks closed. The last real use of the dock had been in the Second World War, with small naval vessels crowding it. For most of its existence the Albert Dock was only used by Dock Board vessels and small ships waiting for other berths. The rescue of the dock from dereliction in the 1980s seems to have made a silk purse from what in shipping terms was always a sow's ear. Today the dock is one of the major tourist attractions in Britain.

Albert Dock is about people now, rather than ships or cargoes, and any brandy trade is strictly retail.

The dock is named after the man who opened it, Prince Albert Francis Charles Augustus Emmanuel, the consort of Queen Victoria. Born on 26 August 1819 he was the second son of the Duke of Saxe-Coburg-Gotha, and a cousin of Queen Victoria, to whom he was married on 16 February, 1839. He rapidly acquired an excellent command of the English language and of British law and history. He gained the respect of the people of the country by heading Royal Commissions, the Society for Improving the Condition of the Working Classes, the Royal Agricultural Society and the Great Exhibition amongst many other causes. He was a great believer in improved education for all and in the advantages to be gained through science. He carried out the official opening of the Albert Dock on the

Royal yacht 'Fairy' and attended a banquet for 1,000 people in his honour in the warehouses on 30 July, 1846. Prince Albert was also responsible for such things as the popularisation of Christmas trees in this country and many feel that it was Albert who laid the foundations of Britain's respect for the monarchy. He died on 14 December 1861.

Alexandra Dock

Opened 1881

Transferring bulk grain to barges in Alexandra, using a floating elevator.

A spine dock constructed with three branches, good railway connections and the latest and best cargo handling equipment, Alexandra Dock was described by Picton as "one of the largest in the world". Its usefulness, however, was limited by the need to enter via the shallow and inconvenient Canada Basin and Langton Dock. Once the entrance problems were sorted out, Alexandra was well positioned to move into bulk trades. Large ships could now enter and berth here, including those of PSNC, Lamport and Holt and Cunard, and there was room to erect the facilities to store bulk goods - massive granary silos for 110,000 tons of grain with floor space for another 20,000 tons. At the end of No.3 Branch Dock The Union Cold Storage Company built the largest cold store in Europe, with a capacity of no less than 2,668,000 cubic feet. It also provided a direct transfer facility to vessels in No.2 Branch. The Royal Seaforth Dock has now taken much of the bulk trade, but Alexandra remains an important general cargo berth for the Port with some facility for bulk left in Branches 1 and 2.

Alexandra is still a centre for bulk handling.

The original intention was for this dock to be named Atlantic Dock and it was known as such for almost a year during its construction. It would appear that this name was not to the liking of the Princess of Wales and when the Prince of Wales opened the dock it was called the Alexandra Dock, after the Princess, "being the name given to it by her Royal Highness, the Princess of Wales". The daughter of Princess Louise and Prince Christian of Schleswig-Holstein-Sonderburg-Glucksberg who eventually ascended the Danish throne, Alexandra was born on 1

December 1844. She married the Prince of Wales, Albert Edward, later Edward VII, on 10 March 1863. With the almost complete retirement of Queen Victoria from public life during her protracted period of mourning, the Prince and Princess of Wales became popular and there was some pressure for the Queen to abdicate in their favour. Alexandra and Edward had six children including the future George V. Alexandra did a great deal of work for charities dealing with the poor, unemployed and underprivileged - setting up, for example, the Queen Alexandra Imperial Military Nursing Service in 1902. On Edward's death in May 1910, Alexandra, now Queen Mother, increased her interest in charity work, particularly during the First World War, setting the standard for Royal involvement in charitable causes which has continued down to the present day. Alexandra died on 20 November, 1925.

Alfred Dock

Commenced 1862 Opened 1866 Altered 1926-9

A grab dredger at work in Alfred c. 1900.

The problems of the Low Water Basin (q.v.) and his total conviction that it would never work led to John Bernard Hartley producing plans in 1856 for an alternative entrance to the Great Float. This consisted of the 'Intermediate' dock entered by three locks and divided from the Great Float by another series of locks. The intermediate dock, later named Alfred, lacked many of the facilities of a 'real' dock, being only a glorified entrance basin, though sheds were later erected on the north and south quays and ships did berth there. The main use of the dock was as part of the Northern or Alfred Entrances, the main access to the Birkenhead system from the river. Originally built with three entrance locks of 30, 50 and 100 feet widths, the 30 and 50 foot entrances were combined into one 80 foot wide deeper entrance in 1926-9. This new entrance was a foot deeper than the old Low Water Basin but was much more easily maintained, being so much narrower. The entrance gates were powered hydraulically from the Tower Road power centre and an accumulator tower to store that power was built on the island between the outer entrances. The dock sheds were pressed into service as part of the Foreign Animals Wharf for a period but were mainly used for general cargoes. After the demolition of the sheds the sides of the dock became the hosts to extensive scrap metal businesses. With the closure of the Morpeth entrances the Alfred Dock became the only entrance into the Birkenhead system and will remain operational as long as the Birkenhead docks, which are now enjoying a revival of traffic, do.

Alfred is still the entrance for the whole of the Birkenhead system. Notice in the foreground that J. B. Hartley's granite copings are still in service.

The dock is named after Prince Alfred, Duke of Edinburgh who opened the dock and the Northern Entrances on 21 June 1866. Prince Alfred Ernest Albert was born on the 6 August, 1844, the second son of Queen Victoria and Prince Albert. He was an appropriate choice to open the Dock, as his rise in the Navy had been meteoric. Joining in 1858, he was commissioned Lieutenant by 1863, 1866 Captain (missing the rank of Commander), 1878 Rear Admiral, 1879 Commander Naval Reserve, 1882 Vice Admiral, 1887 Admiral. In 1893 he was Admiral of the Fleet before he was fifty. Despite a hint of nepotism - he reached admiral with seven years less service than Nelson - he was apparently a very skilled officer. On the Queen's birthday (24 May) just prior to performing the ceremonials at Alfred Dock, he had been invested with the following titles: Duke of Edinburgh, the Earldoms of Ulster and Kent, the Orders of the Garter, the Thistle and St. Patrick, the Grand Cross of the Bath, St. Michael and St. George, the Star of India and of the Indian Empire and a number of foreign orders. In 1893, on the death of his uncle, he added the Duchy of Saxe Coburg Gotha to his collection. He had married the Grand Duchess Marie Alexandrovna, the only daughter of Tsar Alexander II of Russia in January 1874. The couple had four children. Alfred died suddenly on 30 July 1900.

Bidston Dock

Opened 1933

Discharging timber at Bidston when the dock was barely completed.

Long planned as an eventual extension of the Great Float to the other side of the Halfpenny or Poulton Bridge onto the marshland of Bidston Moss, Bidston Dock was finally built in the1930 s. Extensive alterations were carried out in the 1950s to provide specialist berths for the handling of bulk iron ore bound for the Shotton steelworks of John Summers and Co. Special cranes were erected on the dockside for the lifting of large quantities of ore from ships. The decline of the British steel industry and the closure of both the Shotton steel works and of the plant that had been erected at Bidston to take advantage of the ready source of imported ore led to a serious decline in the amount of ore coming across the Bidston quays in the 1970s. The original plan for the dock allowed for an extension further into the Moss if pressure of business made it necessary but it never came about and today the cranes stand idle. Bidston was always the most inconvenient dock to reach - requiring the opening of three bridges and today is only used by occasional roll on - roll off vessels and for long term berthing of ships, for example, Isle of Man Steam Packet ships laid up over winter.

The Dock obviously owes its name to the nearby village of Bidston. The derivation of the name of the village itself, however, is not so clear, seemingly being related to a rock feature or rock with a dwelling near to it.

The iron ore transporters standing idle, summer 1992

11

Bramley Moore Dock

Opened 1848   Closed 1988

Floating coal elevators (used for bunkering ships) loading at the High Level Coal Railway.

Long, rectangular, and the most northerly dock in 1848, Bramley Moore began life as home to the larger steamers of the day. These were quickly taken up by Sandon and Huskisson, and Bramley Moore became home to the Liverpool Docks coal export and bunkering service. Huge quantities of coal were exported from Britain in the nineteenth century and the growing numbers of steamers created a need for quick loading of coal, whether as cargo or fuel. The high level coal railway was created to fill this need, being simply an elevated railway run by the Lancashire and Yorkshire Railway Company, along which wagon loads of coal could be run and subsequently dumped into a ship. It ran with diminishing success from 1856 to 1966, by which time nearly all ships used either diesel engines or oil-fired steam turbines, so that bunker coal was no longer required. At the same time, British coal exports had become insignificant. Bramley Moore for much of its existence was almost a single-traffic dock, although its south quay was popular with companies in the Mediterranean trades.

South Bramley Moore still has a small amount of commercial traffic - notice the refurbished shed in the background

The Dock was named after and opened by John Bramley Moore, Chairman of the Dock Committee, on 4 August 1848, together with the Salisbury, Collingwood, Stanley and Nelson Docks. Born as John Moore in Leeds in 1800, he made his money trading to Brazil. Moore lived for several years in Rio de Janeiro, marrying Seraphina Pennell, the daughter of the British Consul General in 1830. In 1835 he returned to England settling in

Liverpool to run his mercantile interests. In 1841 he was elected Alderman by the Town Council, and remained so until 1865. Also in 1841, Moore became a member of the Dock Committee and assumed the name Bramley Moore. The next year he was Chairman of the Dock Committee and his drive would give vital support for the port's expansion - backing Hartley and negotiating the purchase of much of the land for the northern extensions from the Earls of Derby. In 1846, at the opening of the Albert Dock, he was offered a knighthood, but refused it. In 1848 he was Mayor of Liverpool. He was Conservative M.P. for Maldon in the late 1850s and for Lincoln between 1862-65. He had stood for Liverpool in 1853, but was not elected. Bramley Moore died in Brighton on 19 November 1886 and was brought back to Liverpool for burial at St. Michael's in the Hamlet, Toxteth Park.

Brocklebank Dock.

Built 1862, named 1879. Frequently altered.

Building the new ferro-concrete sheds at Brocklebank in 1907

Brocklebank Dock started life as the Canada half-tide entrance basin (see Canada Dock). It had two branch docks, which, unusually, did not share its name, being know as North and South Carriers Docks respectively. These branches, which extended back almost to the dock road, were intended, like Chester Basin and Manchester Basin (q.v.). for the use of river goods carriers. Initially, the main cargo was timber, but the alterations to Canada and Langton Docks brought about extensive changes, including the shape of Brocklebank. In 1898, South Carriers Dock was converted into a graving dock. By the 1920s, a modernisation programme had provided effective new sheds equipped with electric cranes, and the dock was home mainly to Houlder Bros. (trading to South America) and Commonwealth Government Lines (Australia). In 1958 the dock was again reconstructed in connection with the new Langton Entrance. and its main uses today are for roll on-roll off berths and for accommodation for the MD&HC Marine Operations Division.

Discharging timber at Carriers Dock before its incorporation into Brocklebank.

The Dock is named after Ralph Brocklebank, who was Chairman of MD&HB from 1863-69. Born in 1803, Ralph Brocklebank moved to Liverpool in 1826 to join the family firm of T & J Brocklebank. He was elected to the Dock Committee in 1851 and to the Board on its establishment, retiring in 1883 at the age of 80. He was also a Director of the Royal Insurance Company and was a prominent supporter of a number of charitable institutions including the schoolship Conway, the Liverpool Homes for Aged Mariners and the Sailor's Home. It was in 1879 that Canada Half-Tide was re-named in his honour, and he died on 2 February 1892.

The MD&HC depot at West Brocklebank.

Brunswick Dock

Opened 1832 Branch Dock 1878 Alteration 1905 Closed 1975

The granaries at Coburg and Brunswick saw the last traffic in the South Docks.

A large dock of 12½ acres, built specifically for the accommodation of the timber trade. A special timber quay sloping down into the water of the dock to facilitate the unloading of wood from the timber ships was provided on the east side of the dock. These vessels had an equivalent of the modern bow door, which enabled them to discharge long baulks directly onto the low level quay, and timber could also be dropped overside (as in the timber ponds used in many other ports) and retrieved at the low quay. The timber trade had long been an important part of Liverpool's commerce, and remains so today. Used for local building and shipbuilding initially, the timber went to supply the needs of much of the north and west of England and Wales. Originally the timber was hauled ashore on the beach at what became Queens Dock, then on the quay of Queens. Although it was Liverpool's biggest dock to date, Brunswick soon proved insufficient for the

18

rapidly growing needs of the timber trade. At the end of the 1850s, ships carrying timber were being delayed an average of thirty days in the river, and new facilities were built to the north, particularly at Canada Dock, and across the Mersey in the Great Float. The sloping quays were removed in 1873 and a branch dock added in 1878. The dock was no longer deep enough for the largest ocean-going vessels, but now provided a home for the ships that traded to the ports of West Africa and South America, which had poor harbours and could only accommodate fairly shallow-draught vessels. During A. G. Lyster's great modernisation programme at the beginning of this century it was deepened considerably. In 1937 the opening of a granary at Brunswick led to large numbers of grain ships using it, and Brunswick was the last of the south docks to close, remaining open for grain ships until 1975. The granary remained open for another decade, taking its deliveries by road from Seaforth before being demolished in 1988.

This dock appears to have two separate justifications for its name. The first, and obvious, one is after New Brunswick (Canada) whence much of the timber came. The second, more political, one is after the House of Brunswick, as a conspicuous symbol of Liverpool's support for the 'wronged' Queen Caroline Amèlia Elizabeth of Brunswick-Wolfenbüttel, wife of George IV. Caroline was born on 17 May 1768, and was George's cousin being the daughter of the Duke of Brunswick and Princess Augusta of England, the sister of George III. The Duke of York, during war service in France, had spent time with the Duke of Brunswick and met Caroline, marking her as a likely bride for his brother the Prince of Wales. King George III, anxious to ensure the hereditary line of succession, pressurised the Prince into marriage. The Prince agreed to the match - on condition that his income was doubled to over £125,000 a year. The marriage took place in April 1795, with Prince George receiving tens of thousands of pounds for preparations, jewels and so on. George was rumoured to have been paralytic drunk on his wedding night, but in January 1796, the couple nevertheless had a daughter, Charlotte Augusta. Almost immediately the Prince returned to his old life-style and three months later he announced his wish for a separation. For the next twenty years the Prince treated his wife in an extremely shabby manner. Despite his own life-style (see Princes Dock) his supporters accused Caroline of having affairs, resulting in an investigation by a committee of Lords appointed by the King, denied her access to her daughter and generally denied her the status of the wife of the heir to the throne. The general dislike of the Prince and his treatment of his wife made Caroline a figure of popular sympathy. When a bill of 1820 to remove her title of Queen on her husband's succession and to dissolve their marriage was withdrawn from the House of Commons, a procession of 35,000 people is said to have taken place in Liverpool with church bells ringing and general celebration. When George was to be crowned in July 1821, the Queen was refused entrance to the ceremony. She did not force the issue fearing a popular riot. She died soon after in August 1821. Having expressed a desire to be buried in Brunswick, the King wished her remains to avoid the City of London. However, after an encounter between the people of London and the Life-Guards, the funeral passed through the city. Caroline was laid to rest in her home soil.

There is still plenty of demand for berths at Brunswick, but not for discharging grain.

Canada Dock

Opened 1859

Jesse Hartley's astonishing neo-mediaval pumping station at Canada entrance

Jesse Hartley's last and biggest dock, with a water area (in its original form) of 18 acres. It was built to provide specialist discharge and storage berths for timber imports, taking over from the grossly overcrowded Brunswick Dock to the South. The location at the extremity of the system was chosen because timber berths were a considerable fire hazard. A fire at Canada in 1893 caused damage worth £50,000, and the glow of the flames was visible as far away as Llandudno. Canada half-tide basin (later Brocklebank Dock), was added in 1862 by G.F. Lyster. The entrance was by a tidal basin and a vast 100ft wide passage. But these had been designed with bulky but shallow paddle steamers in mind, and when greater depth became necessary problems arose which lasted for almost the next hundred years.

The entrance lock was wrongly sited, so that the prevailing winds and tides made entering a risky business at most times. A sluicing system to keep the basin free of silt followed the tradition of large scale sluicing systems on the Mersey by not working. (See Great Low Water Basin) Extensive work in the 1890s alleviated the difficulties to some extent, but the entrance problem was only really solved by complete reconstruction - involving the abolition of the tidal basin - after the second world war. Apart from the entrances, Canada Dock was still a highly useful dock, moving into North American passenger trades with such lines as Cunard. In 1896 and 1903 branch docks were added, and in 1899 a graving dock. Canada Dock remains an important part of the system, with a roll on - roll off (ro-ro) berth, and facilities for bulk oil and general cargoes.

The Mersey Mammoth *floating crane using her huge reach to load construction plant for export from Canada, 1992.*

The dock is named Canada after the major source of the timber that it was built to receive.

Canning Dock

begun 1737, Altered 1829 Closed to Commerce 1972

A sadly damaged negative, but it provides a fine impression of Canning Dock c. 1912.

The entrance to the Old Dock was improved at the time of the Salthouse Dock construction (under the Dock Act of 1737) into a tidal basin to provide a sheltered entrance for both docks. This basin had no outer gates and so would empty of water at low tide and was known as the Dry Dock for this reason. The basin had an area of 4½ acres and also provided access to three graving docks. Like other tidal basins on the Mersey, this one proved unsatisfactory in operation and in 1829 it was fitted with outer gates. A half tide entrance basin was constructed in 1845 and the two were renamed Canning Dock and Basin respectively. The infilling of the Old Dock and the construction of Albert substantially altered Canning. The conversion of the basin to a wet dock obviously greatly increased its utility and it soon came into use for general cargo and acquired transit sheds along its quays. The Canning graving docks and half tide basin are today important elements of the Merseyside Maritime Museum, holding parts of the Museum's ship collection.

The dock was named in tribute to George Canning in 1832. Born in London on 11 April 1770 and educated at Eton and Christ Church, Oxford, Canning was trained as a lawyer, but his main career was to be in politics. In 1794 he was elected as Tory Member of Parliament for Newport, beginning his rise to political power. In 1804 he was appointed Treasurer of the Navy, in 1807 Foreign Minister. In 1812 he was prevailed upon to stand for election as MP for Liverpool and was returned to Parliament. He served as MP for Liverpool until 1823 when he retired upon taking up the post of Foreign Secretary. He then stood in the southern seat of Harwich, becoming Prime Minister in April 1827 and taking the portfolio of Chancellor of the Exchequer at the same time. He died on 8 August 1827. Three thousand guineas were raised for a statue of Canning for the Liverpool Town Hall in view of his contributions to the representation of the town in Parliament particularly in his role as an advocate of Free Trade and in the relaxation of the Corn Laws. These actions which had materially benefited Liverpool commerce, together with his death during the course of the alterations, made the name of Canning the natural choice for the new dock.

Canning Half-Tide in its new role as a tourist facility.

Chester Basin

Opened 1795 Filled 1928-36

Chester Basin in its declining years.

Chester Basin was built for the use of canal boats and Mersey flats using the Chester and Ellesmere Canal (later part of the Shropshire Union) that entered the river at Ellesmere Port. A tidal basin of just 2568 square yards, it provided initially important access to the centre of Liverpool for the enormous armada of small craft that plied their trade across and along the Mersey and up the canals that connected the port to the Midlands and Lancashire. The growth of reliable road and rail facilities in the nineteenth century somewhat reduced the canal trade and the provision of facilities inside the main docks for the smaller vessels greatly reduced the use of Chester basin. The small vessels continually travelling to and from this basin also obstructed the ferry traffic at the landing stage. The dock was filled in with spoil excavated from the first Mersey Road Tunnel.

The basin's name, originally the Chester and Ellesmere Basin from the company that made the most use of it in its early days, indicates the direction of most of its trade. Chester itself is of course named from *castrum*, the Latin word for a military camp, from its origin as a Roman legionary fort.

The 'patch' in the river wall at the extreme right marks the position of the former Chester Basin.

Clarence Dock

Opened 1830   Filled 1929

Clarence Half-Tide in 1928: not so much obsolete as a time-capsule.

Originally built well separated from the main body of the docks to isolate the newly appearing steamships with their risks of fire to other vessels. When built, the closest dock to it was the Princes entrance basin. Expanding demand and increasing use of steamers led to the 'ghetto' quickly being swallowed up, with Waterloo, Victoria and Trafalgar linking it with the rest of the system. Originally Clarence had its own half-tide entrance basin, which it came to share with later docks. Clarence remained almost unaltered until the site was sold off to the Liverpool Corporation for £339,000 as a site for their new power station. Built as a 'ghetto', it remained unaltered for almost a hundred years, handling mostly coastal traffic after its short- lived initial role as the home of the latest steamers. The Clarence Dock Power Station provided power for much of Liverpool, using coal brought into Trafalgar Dock. It closed when superseded by more cost effective national grid power stations, and to reduce pollution from the three huge chimneys that still form a prominent feature of the Mersey skyline.

Clarence Graving Docks are still in use. The remains of the power station beyond indicate the former position of the dock itself.

The dock is named for William, Duke of Clarence, the son of George III and Queen Charlotte, who became William IV. He was born on 21 August 1765. At the age of thirteen, he was sent to sea as an able seaman. He took part in the relief of Gibraltar in 1780 and was rated as a midshipman. William became a friend of Nelson in 1782 while both were stationed in New York. By April 1786 he had reached the rank of Captain, with his own ship, the frigate 'Pegasus', serving with Nelson in the West Indies. In

May 1789 he was created Earl of Munster and Duke of Clarence, and in December appointed Rear Admiral, marking the end of his active service afloat. As the second son of the King, he did not expect to ascend the throne and spent several years in Europe in "entanglements with young women", scrapes and gambles, and in 1790 began an affair with the actress Mrs. Jordan which scandalized Society for years. He was appointed Admiral of the Fleet in 1811 which was meant to be an honorary appointment, but he took it seriously, even putting to sea in command of the Channel Fleet. With the Queen he had two children who died in infancy, but ten with Mrs. Jordan. He died on 20 June 1837 having been determined to live long enough for his niece Princess Victoria to attain her majority, as he had always despised the Duchess of Kent who would have been appointed Regent.

Coburg Dock

Named 1840 Enlarged 1858 Enlarged 1902 Closed 1972

East Side, Coburg Dock 1890 or'91. Note that the Dock Road is in the background: the buildings in the foreground were demolished for quay widening and the building of the overhead railway.

The origins of Coburg Dock go back to the Union Half Tide Basin giving entrance to Queens Dock, built c.1820, and the Brunswick Tidal Basin giving access to Union and Brunswick, opened in 1823. In 1840 the Brunswick Basin was fitted with a set of gates and renamed Coburg. The new gates were 70' wide, which allowed the new wet dock to receive ocean going paddle steamers. This led to a period when both Coburg and Brunswick Docks were the home for American mail packets and liners. From 1842 the dock was also important as the site of the South Dockyard, headquarters for Hartley's construction and repair activities. The enlargement and combination of Coburg and Union produced a bigger dock, but improvements to the north docks led to the liners relocating. The dock had some importance as a repair berth and for grain discharge, with a silo capacity of 62,000 tons. In 1889 an impounding station was opened to increase the water level in the South Docks. By 1931 the South Docks were no longer readily accessible to really large ships due to sandbanks in the river and their generally small entrances, so the impounding station was decommissioned and the South Docks as a whole became used by medium and small sized vessels, which did not need the extra depth of water.

The fitting of the gates to the Brunswick Half Tide Basin in 1840 and the marriage of Queen Victoria to Prince Albert of Saxe-Coburg-Gotha in February of that year, was seen as the perfect opportunity to rename the dock Coburg in honour of the new Prince Consort (see Albert Dock).

New uses for Coburg Dock.

Collingwood Dock

Opened 1848.

What do you think of the booklet so far? The Corporation rubbish berth at NE Collingwood. (City Engineers Department.)

Collingwood Dock is one of five opened in 1848. It was intended from the outset to accommodate only comparatively small vessels, and as ship sizes increased it became suitable only for coasters. It has never been significantly modernised, and its walls and passages are just as Jesse Hartley left them. It was for many years the home of the Liverpool Corporation refuse boats.

The dock is named for Cuthbert Collingwood, Admiral and First Baron Collingwood who was Horatio Nelson's right hand man. Born in 1758, he entered the navy at the age of eleven. Put ashore in command of a landing party of sailors at the Battle of Bunker Hill in 1775 during the American Revolution, he was promoted to Lieutenant. In 1778 he was posted as First Lieutenant on the 'Lowestoft', of which Nelson was the Captain. The two rose together to head the British Atlantic Fleet. From 1797 Collingwood had the job of blockading the French and Spanish Fleets within their harbours from Cape St. Vincent to Trafalgar, and at the climactic battle of Trafalgar in 1805, he led the Lee Division and was created a Baron for his part in the victory.

The view across Collingwood to Stanley gives a good impression of the vast size of the tobacco warehouse.

Dukes Dock

Opened 1773 Closed 1972

Not the middle of Manchester: Duke's Dock in the early years of this century.

One of the important stimuli to the development of both Liverpool and Manchester was the route between the two towns provided by the Duke of Bridgewater's canal. This canal linked the Duke's coal mines at Worsley with Manchester, the Trent and Mersey Canal, and in 1773 the Mersey itself at Runcorn. In order to unload the canal barges near the centre of Liverpool a long narrow basin was built which was called Dukes Dock. Probably built to the design of James Brindley, the engineer who built the Bridgewater canal, this featured a warehouse which was built in 1783 over spurs from the basin and allowed for the easy unloading of vessels straight into storage. This was the first dockside warehouse on Merseyside. The Bridgewater canal itself was a notable pioneer as it was the first English canal to depart substantially from an existing watercourse. All previous 'canals' in this country had been designed as navigations i.e. improvements to natural watercourses to make them deep enough for canal boats. The

Dukes Dock was extended in the 1790s as the trade between Liverpool and Manchester grew on the basis of the burgeoning cotton industry. Until 1900, the Dock had remained the property of the successors to the Duke's estate, ultimately the Manchester Ship Canal Co., but in that year it was finally purchased by MD&HB. The warehouses stood until 1960.

The new pedestrian footbridge over Duke's Dock.

The dock is named for Francis Egerton, the third and last Duke of Bridgewater. Born in 1736 the Duke retired from London social life to his estates at Worsley after breaking off his engagement to the Duchess of Hamilton. He worked on the development of his mines and in order to move the coal he produced to its markets he constructed the canal that bears his name, with the aid of James Brindley, the famous engineer, and John Gilbert, his agent. The success of the canal and the money he earned from tolls and from diversification into other fields made him an immensely wealthy man. His experience with the Duchess seems to have turned him into something of a misogynist as he never married and he refused to allow a woman to even wait upon him. His death on 3 March 1803 was the signal for eulogies calling him the 'first great Manchester man,' and recognising his pivotal role in the growth of both Liverpool and Manchester.

Egerton Dock

Commenced 1844 Opened 1847 Filled 1991

*Egerton was never the biggest or the best. The arched walling is,
however, unusual in dockbuilding practice on the Mersey.*

The second Egerton Dock on the Mersey (see Harrington Dock for more
details of the first one). Egerton dock owed its origin to the Birkenhead
Docks scheme organised by a group of local business magnates of whom
the best known was John Laird (see Wallasey Dock for more on this
scheme). Too small even from the start, its original intent as an entrance to
an arm of the Low Water Basin was forgotten as the Birkenhead scheme
lurched from one disaster to another. Throughout its working life it mainly
served the railway companies such as the London and North Western and

Cheshire Lines Committee whose stations abutted it. The LNWR built a warehouse on the south quay which served as a banana shed for much of its existence.

Egerton Dock is named after Sir Philip de Malpas-Grey Egerton who performed the ceremonies of laying the foundations to Birkenhead Docks in 1844. Born at Oulton Park, Tarporley, Cheshire on 13 November 1806, and educated at Eton and Christ Church, Oxford, he was interested in science, particularly geology, being a fellow of the Geological Society, the Royal Society and a member of the councils of both societies and a trustee of the British Museum and the Royal College of Surgeons. The main aim of the Birkenhead Dock Trustees in naming the Dock after him was however to attempt to secure his political influence in the extensive parliamentary disputes with the Liverpool Corporation which was, not surprisingly, hostile to competition on the Cheshire bank of the Mersey. Sir Philip became Tory MP for Chester and apart from a brief hiatus between 1832 and 1835 represented Southern Chester or West Cheshire until his retirement.

Not a transit shed; the cut-down remains of the LNWR warehouse.

Georges Dock

Opened 1771 Reconstructed 1822-5 Filled 1900

The view across Georges Dock from the end of Irwell Street in the 1880's.

The third of the Liverpool docks, begun in 1762 to the north of the previously existing Old and South Docks and therefore initially called North Dock. The increase in the number of ships using the port coupled with the clear advantages given by wet docks in the unloading of ships made more docks a desirable aim and work commenced in 1762 under Henry Berry as dock engineer. The dock as originally constructed covered a area of a little over three acres. Initially serving vessels in the North American and Caribbean trades, it lost these to Princes Dock in 1821 and was then heavily reconstructed and almost doubled in size. On the eastern (landward) side of the dock were the Goree warehouses which are very obvious on marine paintings of the time. These were built in 1793 and devastated by the well known fire of 1802 which caused damage valued at over £320,000 and was instrumental in the introduction of a local building act to reduce the vulnerability of commercial buildings. After the extension to the dock and the construction of steamer docks to the north Georges Dock was mainly left to schooners carrying fruit and other perishables.

The passage from Canning used to lead through to Georges.

To the west of the dock the land initially occupied by timber yards was soon formed into a small gun battery and two basins for ferries which provided cross river communication. These were superseded by the landing stage in 1847 which was extended and modernised in 1874 immediately prior to an immense blaze which necessitated major repairs. The works of 1874 involved the infilling of Georges Dock Basin, which disappeared under the floating roadway and St Nicolas Place. On the land between dock and stage were constructed the town baths in 1829. The dock was filled in 1900 to provide the land for a major exercise in civic pride as the Liver, Cunard and Dock Board Office (now Port of Liverpool) buildings were erected on the site in the first decade of the century to produce the best known waterfront in the world.

The dock was named for the reigning monarch at the time of its opening, King George III, grandson of George II. Born on 4 June, 1738, George became Prince of Wales in 1751 on the death of his father Frederick. George and his wife Charlotte were crowned on 22 September 1761. The diamond fell from the King's crown after the ceremony. This was later pointed out as an ominous sign when the King's madness began to manifest itself. George's reign was marked by considerable constitutional conflict brought about by a perceived attempt to extend the powers of the Crown, and he played a personal role in bringing about the American War of Independence. Despite his loss of the American colonies and growing symptoms of lunacy - his conversation with an oak tree which he had mistaken for the King of Prussia is legendary - he retained a certain popularity in middle class circles. By 1805 he was almost blind and by 1811 the Regency Bill established his son as the Prince Regent. He died on 29 January 1820, after sixty years on the throne.

Gladstone Dock

Opened 1927

Towards the end of the break-bulk cargo handling era, Gladstone in 1963.

Despite a series of arguments that it would be too large for the needs of the port, the Gladstone Dock was sanctioned in 1908. Consisting of an entrance dock and two branch docks with 58¼ acres of water space, three miles of quays, single, double and even triple story transit sheds, electric cranes and connected directly to railway goods yards, Gladstone Dock dragged the Port of Liverpool into the twentieth century and went some way towards alleviating the difficulties the post war period would bring. The largest entrance lock on the river, 1070 feet (326m) long, 130 feet (39.6m) wide, enabled any ship then afloat or on the drawing board to enter, and thus greatly improved the usefulness of Brocklebank, Langton, Alexandra and Hornby, through bypassing the troublesome Canada Basin. The graving dock, the first element of the system completed, opened in

1913, was only slightly smaller than the lock and was to more than prove its value in both World Wars. The Cunard liner 'Aquitania' was in the graving dock when World War I broke out, and was quickly converted into an armed merchant cruiser. The First World War, with its associated labour shortages, forced delay in construction of the rest of the system, though work was restarted using German prisoners of war in 1917. The dock was fully opened in 1927. While originally built for the old style of labour- intensive piecemeal cargo handling, the size of the dock and the amount of land round it, made it readily adaptable to new methods. The huge entrance would prove to be invaluable, as it is still in use today, serving not only Gladstone Dock but also the Royal Seaforth Dock and Container Terminal.

Contrary to popular opinion, the dock is not named after Prime Minister William Ewart Gladstone, but after his second cousin, Robert Gladstone, a Liverpool merchant. In association with the royal visit for the opening, it was proposed to include 'Royal' in the name of the dock. Royal Dock, Royal George Dock and Royal Mary's Dock were all suggested, but eventually it was decided to follow the precedent of Hornby and Brocklebank by naming it in honour of the Chairman of the Board who had played a large part in ensuring that the dock came to be built.

Robert Gladstone was born in Abercromby Square on 17 July 1833, and educated at Eton and Edinburgh University. In 1850 he married Mary Ellen Gladstone, a distant relative, (daughter of Robertson Gladstone, brother of W.E.) who bore him four sons and five daughters. In 1852 - still only 19 years of age - he went to St Petersburg as an assistant with a firm of Russian merchants, where he remained until the outbreak of the Crimean War made continued residence in Russia uncongenial. He travelled around Europe and returned to Liverpool in 1856, joining his father's firm of Gladstone and Sergeantson, who were merchants in the Indian, Chinese and Far Eastern trades. He was elected to the MD&HB in 1881. Throughout his life he was heavily involved in local causes, including the establishment of the University. He played a key role in the planning of the Cathedral, and was the main advocate of its location on St. James Mount. He retired from the Dock Board in 1911 after making a distinguished contribution to the improvement of its ways of conducting business, and was awarded the Freedom of the City the same year. He died at his home in Woolton on 12 July 1919.

Gladstone now handles large amounts of low sulphur coal, imported to reduce the pollution from power stations.

The Great Float

Opened 1851-60

The old 87 ton crane loading locomotives for export to India.

The main feature of the Birkenhead Docks scheme, both in size and usefulness, was the huge dock formed by impounding Wallasey Pool. The engineer James Meadows Rendel intended this to provide a reservoir of water to power the sluicing system to clear the Low Water Basin (q.v.) and also to serve as a "highway" giving access to docks that were to be built along its margins. The series of changes of plan during the construction of the docks led to an altering of emphasis in the purpose of the Great Float from being a "highway" to being a dock in itself, with a water area of over 110 acres, and more than four miles of quayside. The East Float from Duke Street bridge to the entrances was usable in 1851 but many of the walls, particularly on the north side, were only part finished. The take-over by the MD&HB led to the West Float up to the Poulton Bridge and the rest of the East Float becoming operational in 1860. The quays of the Float

were now serving as berth space and it would be the next century before
any docks were built leading off the Float. The Float handled a wide
variety of cargoes as befits a 'dock' of its size. Emigrants travelled to
Australia in the 1850s from the East Float, coaling appliances were used to
fuel steamers, limestone and guano arrived to provide raw materials for
cement and fertilisers in the dockside factories, grain came to the mills of
the flour companies, ships were repaired in the graving docks and the Float
was the centre of a vast hive of industry. Until the opening of the Vittoria
Dock it is only a slight exaggeration to say that the Great Float *was*
Birkenhead docks - by far the greatest proportion of the trade of the system
passed over the quays of the Float.

The name is due to the original function of the dock - to serve as a reservoir
for sluicing and as a 'floating dock' where vessels would remain afloat i.e. a
wet dock as opposed to a dry dock. A second, quite separate, justification
sometimes offered is that timber was discharged overside into the water
here; some docks where that was practised were known as timber floats.
The prefix 'Great' comes simply from its unusual size. Indeed this size was
to result in some confusion in berthing vessels, so it became generally
known by its two ends (divided by the Duke Street Bridge), East Float and
West Float.

This picture shows about half the length of the Great Float!

The 'Great' Low Water Basin

Commenced 1844 'Completed' 1863 Out of use 1866 Converted 1874

We failed to find a photograph of the Great Low Water Basin. We would be interested to hear of the existence of one.

The original entrance to the Birkenhead docks was claimed as a potential triumph of the art and science of dock engineering by James Rendel who designed it. The basin was one of the main features in the continuous outbreaks of recriminations, redesigns and financial problems which plagued the Birkenhead scheme until well after the establishment of the MD&HB. The Birkenhead docks were based on Wallasey Pool. The Low Water Basin was to be basically a 'hole' scooped in this with walls along the side of it, a gate at the inner end and the outer end open to the river. The basin was to have its bottom twelve feet below the low water mark of spring tides. This is very deep for the Mersey and there was a great deal of controversy over whether it would be possible to maintain it at that depth. Rendel proposed a system of sluices using the water from the Great Float to "flush" the basin of accumulated river silt when necessary. In use the scheme was an utter disaster. The change in level in the Great Float ripped vessels from their moorings, broke sluicing paddles, shifted the masonry of the dam at the end of the basin and the bottom of the basin developed into a series of humps and hollows. Sluicing was abandoned in 1864 and silt built up to such an extent that the landing stage in the basin grounded. The basin was eventually converted into Wallasey Dock (q.v.).

The name originates in the purpose of the basin. Great because of its size - it was the largest work of its kind yet attempted - and Low Water because it would be fully accessible to all but the largest vessels of the period at any but the lowest of tides. It was immensely controversial and both Jesse and J.B. Hartley were vehemently against its inclusion in the scheme when the MD&HB took over. The railway companies at Birkenhead, particularly the Great Western, exerted strong pressure to retain the basin as it would enable quick transfer of passengers and goods to their trains from the landing stages in the basin. The scheme was a fiasco.

Harrington Dock

Opened 1882 Closed 1972

Hydraulic roof cranes in use at the two-storey transit sheds at Harrington.

The first dock on this site was Egerton Dock, built by the Bridgewater Trustees in 1837-9. Like Dukes Dock and the Chester and Manchester Basins, this small dock with only a 20' wide entrance, was intended for the use of river and canal craft mainly dealing with timber. In 1839 a private company, largely comprised of Liverpool councillors, employed Jesse and John Hartley to design two further small basins called the Harrington Dock and Harrington Dry Basin on the site. The Harrington Company was not commercially successful, the Bridgewater Trust moved much of their operations northwards and the land was acquired by the Liverpool Dock Trust for future expansion. This expansion eventually came about with the completion of the new Harrington Dock in 1883. It was open for two years before being named, during which time it was succinctly known as "Dock,

North of Herculaneum Half-Tide Dock". The depth of water and width of entrances quickly proved inadequate to the needs of the dock users, and major improvements were made in 1898. For many years, Harrington provided appropriated berths for the Elder Dempster Line and its associated companies.

The dock owes its name to the district of Harrington. The Earl of Sefton, who owned the former Royal Forest of Toxteth Park, laid out the land in 1775 for an extension or overflow town to be called New Liverpool. This name was dropped in favour of 'Harrington' in tribute to his wife who was the daughter of the Earl of Harrington. The name of the district fell into disuse in later years, but it survived to be applied to the dock company, and later still to the new dock. The Egerton Dock was so called from the family name of the Duke of Bridgewater (see Dukes Dock).

A new use for the two storey sheds.

Herculaneum Dock

Opened 1866   Closed 1972   Filled 1974

The graving docks and bunkering berths at Herculaneum were still busy in 1963.

The first dock on the site was a tiny basin used for vessels carrying copper ore to Charles Roe's smelting business in around 1767. The first serious wet dock was mooted here in 1840 by a group of capitalists who later began the Birkenhead Docks scheme. The problems at Birkenhead would result in the company selling the land in 1848 to the Liverpool Dock Committee for future expansion. Work did not begin on the site until 1864, being the first major work by G.F. Lyster as the MD&HB Dock Engineer, though some preliminary work was done by J.B. Hartley before his retirement in 1861. The river entrance and the small Herculaneum Dock were really only adjuncts to the Graving Docks, which were the main object of the exercise. The first two graving docks were opened in 1864, a third in 1876 and a fourth in 1902. Obviously ships only needed to come in and out of the graving docks at irregular intervals, so to make better use of the dock, a new branch was added in 1878. In 1885 an entrance lock was completed, ending half-tide operation.

A similar view in 1992.

Herculaneum is unusual in that most of its area was excavated from dry land: most of the Liverpool docks are built out onto the foreshore. The branch was equipped with "casemates", short tunnels into the rock with heavy doors at their entrances, used for safe storage of petroleum and other explosive and inflammable materials. They are thought to have been the first such specialist facility, and remain to this day. The adjacent land at the Dingle was adopted for oil storage when oil began to arrive in bulk tankers rather than in barrels. Oil tanks, mooring buoys and jetties were built to take oil from ship to shore. This facility was superseded by the Tranmere Terminal across the river in the Sloyne, which supplied oil direct to the Stanlow Refinery. Herculaneum reached its greatest importance in the Second World War when the four graving docks were in almost constant use. The docks and the Dingle oil terminal provided part of the site for the 1984 International Garden Festival.

The dock is named after the business of the Herculaneum Pottery Company which was established on the site in 1796. This final fling of the once-important Liverpool pottery industry came too late to compete effectively with the growth of the Staffordshire potteries on the one hand and of the import trade on the other. The company folded in 1833, being carried on by successors until the land was acquired in 1841 by the speculators of the Herculaneum Dock Company.

Hornby Dock

Opened 1884

Loading a part-cargo of containers at Hornby in 1969 - before the opening of the specialist facilities at Seaforth.

The most northerly dock of the time. It marked the end of the nineteenth century dock expansion and the beginning of a long period of modernisation and refurbishment for the MD&HB. It would be 25 years until the next new dock - the Vittoria in Birkenhead - was built and 43 before the next dock on the Liverpool side - the Gladstone. Hornby was built as part of the huge programme of construction enabled by the 1873 Dock Act, along with Alexandra and Langton, and it shared similar features - transit sheds, cranes, rail access. In its early years, Hornby was mainly used by the timber trade, and it featured a sloping quay like that at Brunswick.

It was always intended to construct further docks northwards from Hornby. Parliamentary powers were obtained in 1906 for the lock between Hornby and what would later be Gladstone. In 1940, that lock was bombed and very badly damaged, creating a major problem for the ships using the docks, which hampered operation right through the war. Today, the Hornby Dock is still operational, handling general cargo and stripping containers.

Hornby continues to attract good traffic - hence the new shed.

Thomas Dyson Hornby was born in Northumberland Terrace, Everton on 1 February 1822 and was educated locally then at Rugby School. He duly joined the family firm of T. & J. H. Hornby, general merchants, and was elected to the MD&HB in April 1862. He served on several committees, and became Chairman in 1876, on the death of William Langton (see Langton Dock), which office he held until his death on 31 July 1889, when he was taken ill while on Board business in London opposing a supplementary bill of the Manchester Ship Canal. Outside of business interests he was an active member of the local Liberal Party and served as a County Magistrate, but was also remembered as a keen sportsman whose dogs competed in the Waterloo Cup and who was a pillar of the Liverpool Cricket Club.

Huskisson Dock

The White Star liner Oceanic *at West Huskisson, 1902.*

In some ways the history of the North Docks can be seen repeated in microcosm in Huskisson Dock. Opened in 1852 for the timber trade, it was extended 50% to the east in 1860 to handle larger vessels in more prestigious trades as the timber moved to Canada Dock. In 1862 the first branch was built. 1892 saw the passage between Canada and Huskisson widened to allow access to the larger vessels of the day. The start of the century saw two further branch docks and the renumbering mentioned in the introduction. The major improvements to Sandon Entrance made Huskisson a desirable place for the North American cargo and passenger trades operated by such lines as Cunard until the opening of the Gladstone entrance. Today, Huskisson still handles general cargo, bulk oil and other bulks.

The dock was named after William Huskisson for his political contributions to the commercial prosperity of Liverpool. Born on 11 March 1770, he was sent to Paris in 1783 to be educated by his great uncle, Doctor Gem, who was physician to the British Embassy. Huskisson was said to have been present at the fall of the Bastille in 1789. In 1792 the British Embassy was recalled and Huskisson put his expertise to use in making arrangements for the emigres fleeing the French Revolution. In 1796 he was elected MP for Morpeth and later served for a succession of southern seats. In 1822 he was made a member of the Board of Trade.

The retirement of Canning (see Canning Dock) as a Liverpool Member of Parliament led to Huskisson being adopted as the only Tory candidate likely to win the approval of the Liverpool merchants. He was duly elected in February 1823 and fiercely represented the town's interests in Parliament, introducing a succession of Bills on such subjects as apprenticeships for merchant seamen, ship registration and sorting out the morass of Customs Laws, reducing duties on cotton, woollen goods, glass and paper, which all benefited the Port of Liverpool. From 1828 his health was failing, but he tragically forced himself from his sick-bed for the opening of the Liverpool and Manchester Railway on 15 September 1830. While standing on the tracks attempting a reconciliation with the Duke of Wellington (with whom he had recently argued), Huskisson was hit by the 'Rocket' locomotive and his leg was run over. He died a few hours later. His constituents raised £3,000 for a statue to him, and eulogies filled the local papers. The naming of the dock after him was a logical tribute to the man.

Kings Dock

**Commenced 1785 Opened 1788 Reconstructed 1901 Closed 1972
Filled 1983**

Kings No. 1 Branch in 1971, looking busy despite having only a year to live.

Constructed to the south of the existing docks to meet the urgent need for additional dock space that would be a recurring theme in the history of the port. The then privately owned Dukes Dock meant that the Kings and the later group of docks that spread south from it remained isolated from the main system until the building of the Wapping basin in 1852. Built at a cost of £25,000 and covering around seven acres the dock displaced many of the shipbuilding yards that were the previous occupants of the site. The

Kings Dock became notable for the presence of the Kings tobacco warehouse, completed 1795. This warehouse, for the bonded storage of imported tobacco played an important role in the securing of a large portion of the lucrative trade for the Mersey and in jobs in local industries. Indeed this warehouse rapidly proved to be too small and was soon replaced by a larger building in 1811 at a cost of £140,000, its predecessor being used for general warehousing. Kings was subjected to extensive reconstructions, being shortened by the Wapping construction programme in the 1850s and both Kings and the neighbouring Queens dock were extensively altered at the beginning of the twentieth century. This alteration produced two branch docks at Kings from a central spine providing more quay space within the same area. Latterly, the dock was mainly used by the Mediterranean fruit trade, for which its quaysides were remodelled as recently as 1966.

The Kings branches are infilled, and form one of the more significant development sites still on offer.

When the South Docks closed in 1972 a period of dereliction was followed by the site clearance and dock filling that has left the Kings Dock as the car-park for the Albert Dock complex and as a site available for future development.

The dock was named for the King at the time, George III, (See Georges Dock.)

Langton Dock

Opened 1881

Installed as part of the 'New North Works' programme completed in 1881,
this crane was for the heaviest indivisible export loads.

Another of the Docks of the great 1873 programme, Langton was partly operational in 1879 and officially opened concurrently with Alexandra Dock in 1881. The layout is of a spine and branch dock, but only one "branch" was a wet dock, the other two being large graving docks which were notable for the excellence of their equipment and the inadequate depth of water over their sills. Langton had been intended for very large vessels, but mainly became home to the Mediterranean trade, including Ellerman Line and John Glynn. Entrance had been via the troublesome Canada Basin, but it was not until 1949 that work began on a new river entrance and even then a series of problems delayed the opening of the new lock until the visit of Her Majesty the Queen on the 14 December, 1962. Today it is still in use in the same general cargo trades that always used it.

William Langton had served on the old Dock Committee, and was elected to MD&HB on its establishment. He was elected Chairman on the retirement of Ralph Brocklebank (see Brocklebank Dock) in 1870. He was a man of many interests: a partner in T. & W. Earle, American merchants, and at various times Chairman of the Bank of Liverpool and of the Pacific Steamship company. His financial expertise was highly respected by contemporaries on the Board and elsewhere, and, being a bachelor, he gave freely to a number of other unpaid calls on his time, including the magistracy, the Treasureship of the Bluecoat School and Liverpool Cricket Club. He died at his home in Abercromby Square on 4 May 1876 at the age of 53. The desire to name a dock after him was strengthened by the fact that he had been Chairman throughout the process of obtaining the Act for the huge 1873 programme of works.

The view across Langton to Brocklebank Branch and the remains of Langton Graving Docks.

Manchester Basin

Opened 1785 Enlarged 1818 Filled 1928-36

Manchester Dock being infilled, 1928.

Manchester Dock began as a small basin operated by the Mersey & Irwell Navigation for the Manchester Trade, and was thus very comparable to Chester Basin. In 1818 it was enlarged and converted from a tidal basin into a half-tide dock. Manchester Dock became most important as a link between the Liverpool and Birkenhead operations of the Great Western Railway (GWR). The GWR had a major goods operation at Birkenhead docks but no direct access to Liverpool, so the transfer of cargo across the river was an important link in their network, enabling them to penetrate the territory of the London & North Western Railway. (which was using Chester Basin and the Shropshire Union Canal to "poach" GWR traffic) The GWR built a warehouse here for the storage of their goods prior to distribution. The dock was filled at the same time as the Chester Basin, but the land continued in use by National Carriers until 1972. The surviving warehouse is now part of the Merseyside Maritime Museum and the

Manchester Dock is now under the Museum's car park. The entrance is still visible in the main river wall, and some of the fill has subsided slightly, making the line of the old basin wall visible in places.

The name is derived from the destination and origin of much of the traffic dealt with at the basin - Manchester. Manchester, like Chester, owes its name to a Roman fortified camp.

The GWR building at Manchester Dock is now restored and forms part of the Merseyside Maritime Museum.

Morpeth Dock

Commenced 1844 Opened 1847 Filled 1990

Restoration work on the sheds of Morpeth Branch, 1992. Some older views would be welcome!

Morpeth Dock was originally designed as a temporary entrance into the developing Birkenhead docks while the main entrance of the system, the Great Low Water Basin, was blocked off by a dam to allow construction. Unfortunately the temporary cut required the removal of large masses of sandstone which the engineers performing the initial survey had totally failed to observe. This proved very expensive and it was decided to turn the cut into a dock. Unfortunately the land used was not the property of the Dock Commission but of the Commissioners of Woods and Forests (who represented the Crown), nor did the Dock Commission did have Parliamentary permission to build. Eventually a swap of land was arranged and the dock was legalised. Originally a long narrow dock, like a large entrance lock, it was very unsatisfactory in use. It was, for example, impossible for any but the smallest of vessels to turn within it. In 1872 it was extensively remodelled with a Branch Dock and a canal basin leading onto the Great Western Railway's goods station. It handled canal and Mersey flat traffic into the GWR station and provided berths for a number of Far Eastern Shipping companies such as the Pacific Steam Navigation Company, Brocklebank's, Bibby and Holt until they moved to the Great Float and Vittoria Dock. The areas once used by the shipping companies then became part of the Woodside cattle lairages. The Branch Dock was very small and inconvenient for ships and became used for projects that needed large amounts of space - it was used for the ventilator tower for the Birkenhead - Liverpool road tunnel in 1934 and for the 1955 water pumping station and is now slowly being filled in after an extension to the effluent pumping station of the Interceptor Sewer scheme, in preparation for redevelopment.

The dock was named after George William Frederick Howard, the seventh Earl of Carlisle, called Lord Morpeth as a courtesy title. (A courtesy title is that given to the heir to a title before he inherits the 'higher' title.) Howard was born on 18 April, 1802 and educated at Eton and Christ Church, Oxford. He attended the coronation of the Russian Tsar in 1826 and while in Russia he was returned as the Whig MP for the "family seat" of Morpeth. He had a distinguished political career serving as Chief Secretary for Ireland and Lord Lieutenant of Ireland. He became Earl of Carlisle on the death of his father in 1849 and died in 1864. His connection with Birkenhead arises from his role in 1846-49 as the Chief Commissioner of Woods and Forests. His co-operation was vital in sorting out the problems over the 'temporary entrance' and as a show of appreciation the Morpeth Dock was named after him, and he opened the Morpeth and Egerton Docks in 1847. He also opened Birkenhead Park, the first publicly funded park in the world, at the same time.

Nelson Dock

Opened 1848

Yo-ho-ho and a tankerful of rum... the pipeline for the former bulk rum trade at Nelson.

Nelson Dock was one of those authorised by the great 1844 Dock Act, of which the first five (including Nelson) were all opened in 1848. Although capable of taking large ships by 1848 standards it was not intended as a "flagship": that role was reserved for the last two docks of the programme, Sandon and Huskisson. Because it was deep and had good entrances in relation to its size, Nelson was always in demand among owners of smaller ships. It last regular trade was in bulk rum (which was piped to the bonded warehouses at Stanley Dock) but it is still in occasional use by coastal container vessels.

The naming of a slightly second-rate dock is not one of the more signal honours accorded to Horatio Nelson, who is generally considered Britain's greatest admiral. Born on 29 September 1758, he entered the navy at the age of twelve under his uncle, Captain Suckling. In 1773 he served on an expedition to the North Pole. In 1776 he was made an Acting Lieutenant, the following year he passed his exams and was commissioned as a Second Lieutenant. In 1780 ill health forced him to retire to Bath. He soon returned to active service in America and the Caribbean. In March 1787 he married Mrs. Nisbet, a widow in the West Indies, with Prince William (see Clarence Dock) giving the bride away. In 1794 he was blinded in the right eye. In 1797 naval successes led to him being appointed Rear Admiral and knighted. He lost his right arm at Santa Cruz, Tenerife later that year. In 1798 after a victory over the French at the Battle of the Nile, he was created Baron Nelson of the Nile. In 1801 at the Battle of Copenhagen, he raised his telescope to his blind eye to avoid seeing his superior's signal to break off the engagement, continued, won and was appointed Vice Admiral. His well known affair with Lady Emma Hamilton began around this time, Nelson separating from his wife and paying the former Mrs. Nisbet an allowance of £1,200 a year. In April 1803 Lord Hamilton died, with his wife smoothing the pillow on one side and Nelson holding his hand on the other. Lady Hamilton and Nelson began to live together and had a daughter Horatia Nelson Thompson. Nelson died at Trafalgar at around 4.30 p.m. on 21 October 1805 with the words: 'Thank God I have done my duty', when victory was assured. His body was brought home preserved in a barrel of spirits and lay in state prior to burial on 9 January 1806.

Growing traffic in the bigger docks to the north has driven some of the smaller vessels back to Nelson.

The Old Dock

Commenced c1709 Opened 1715 Filled 1826

*Jesse Hartley had no consideration for historians: he infilled the Old Dock
before the invention of the camera.*

The first "commercial enclosed wet dock" in the world and the first in the
series of docks that would lay the foundations of Liverpool's commercial
greatness during the nineteenth century. Originally the Port of Liverpool
was based around the Pool, a tidal inlet from the Mersey. In order to keep
the ships afloat and facilitate easy unloading in the town, a dock was built
within the Pool. The small dock of just over 4 ¾ acres would hold over 100
of the ships of the time. The dock was built with brick walls upon wooden
pilings coped with sandstone possibly reused from the then derelict
Liverpool Castle nearby. The dock had a small entrance basin with a
graving dock constructed off it (see Canning Dock). At the same time the
town of Liverpool grew rapidly, with new streets appearing on the
reclaimed land of the upper part of the Pool, and a commercial boom
began.

When constructed it was simply the Dock or the Liverpool Dock. When
more docks were made it became the Old Dock. The small size of the
dock, the way in which later docks cut it off from the river, the health

hazard posed by the enclosed water into which sewers emptied in the middle of town, and the deterioration of the brick walls combined to make it less and less useful. From a time when almost all the trade of Liverpool passed over its quays, the growth of the Port had made it into a minor adjunct which was growing more and more expensive to maintain for a minimal return. Despite this, a combination of sentiment and a desire not to see any reduction in dock accommodation did keep it open for twenty years past its useful life. Filling operations began in 1826 and in 1828 work began on a new Custom House on the site which was lost in the Second World War. The current City Council buildings of Steers House are built on part of the site, named for the engineer, Thomas Steers, who was responsible for the dock.

The 'mismatched' masonry at the left is believe to mark the mouth of the Old Dock.

Princes Dock

Commenced 1810 Opened 1821

The Tower Building and the entrance to Princes Half-Tide.

Eleven years from start to opening marks a series of delays and difficulties caused by such problems as raising money and manpower during the Napoleonic Wars, the acquisition of the port defence battery that occupied part of the prospective site and the mismanagement and fiddling that occurred. Built by the Dock Surveyor John Foster with some preliminary work by William Jessop and John Rennie, the Princes Dock was the largest dock yet constructed on the Mersey, and the flagship of the system built to take the vessels operating in the prestigious and profitable trade to North America. It only spent about twenty years in that primary position before the Jesse Hartley-designed docks to the north stole away much of the American traffic and the dock became home to the high value low bulk Far East and South America trades. Secure transit sheds were erected to handle this trade. By 1910 however, the acquisition of the Birkenhead system and its final completion and improvement had led to much of the South American and Far Eastern traffic moving across the river to Morpeth, Egerton and Vittoria docks, and smaller vessels used the South Docks. Princes had become mainly the centre of the Irish trade. The transatlantic passenger traffic was established on the landing stage in the river and the Riverside railway station was erected in 1895 to handle the transfer of passengers from rail to liner. As trade with Ireland moved into containers Princes Dock became a passenger terminal for Belfast. A roll on-roll off terminal was built at the south end of the dock in 1967 but the decline in passenger service and a new terminal at Victoria Dock led to the service from Princes ending in 1981. The dock today lies empty and unused, awaiting redevelopment.

Named for the Prince Regent, and opened on the day of his Coronation as George IV. George Augustus Frederick was born on the 12 August, 1762, the eldest son of King George III and Queen Charlotte (see Kings and Queens Docks). He soon acquired the reputation of the foremost "gentlemen" of Europe - drinking, gambling, racing, indulging in affairs with a succession of women. He gamed and drank away immense sums of money - £10,000 in 1781 on clothes, £30,000 a year on the maintenance of his stud of racing horses. By 1784 he was £160,000 in debt, but this did not stop him beginning work on the extravagant Brighton Pavilion and enjoying a social life of epic proportions. In 1785 he apparently went through a ceremony of marriage with Mrs. Fitzherbert, a widow. In 1787 he was forced by his growing debts to appeal to Parliament for more money. His supporters assured Parliament that no marriage had taken place and his debts were paid off. In 1788 when King George displayed the first of his bouts of insanity, proposals for the Regency to be given to Prince George were resisted. By 1789 the Prince of Wales was back in debt, pawning his diamonds in 1792. He was almost bribed into his apparently bigamous marriage with Caroline (see Brunswick Dock). When the marriage broke up at his instigation, Mrs. Fitzherbert moved back in. When his father's insanity became seated and he was appointed Regent in February 1811, he threw an expensive celebration and broke his relationship with Mrs. Fitzherbert. While he was clever politically and socially in a number of respects, his conspicuous consumption alienated him from his subjects making him extremely unpopular. 'Bread or the Regent's Head' was a popular slogan in 1816. In 1817 his coach was stoned on his way back from opening Parliament. His coronation in 1821 was a spectacular affair, spending over £50,000 on the crown and £24,000 on his robes alone. This life- style began to show effects on him. After a lifetime of 'good living' he suffered from dropsy and gout, becoming addicted to laudanum to try to ease the pain. By February 1830 he was partially blind and was convinced that he had commanded a division at Waterloo and ridden winners at Goodwood races. He died on 25 June 1830.

The decision thus to name the dock had been taken as early as 1811. It is fairly clear that by 1821 opinions had changed, and the enormous celebrations of the opening were intended as much to upstage the Coronation (which on a local scale they undoubtedly did) as to honour it. Many of the dinners that night featured the nose-thumbing proposal of a toast to Queen Caroline.

Demolition work begun at Princes in 1990.

Queens Dock

**Commenced 1785 Opened 1796 Extended 1816 Altered 1905/6
Closed 1972**

Queens No. 1 Branch, 1903.

Queens Dock was enabled in 1785 under the same Act as Kings, but problems in acquiring and clearing the site led to substantial delay in construction. The new dock shared an entrance basin with the Kings dock and was finally opened in 1796. Smaller than Kings at 5 acres, the construction delays meant it was also more expensive at £35,000. During the delay, Henry Berry, after forty years service, had retired and been replaced by Thomas Morris as dock engineer. The Queens was the only major contribution Morris made to the Liverpool Docks, as he was effectively sacked in 1799. Even the near doubling in size of the dock by a 4½ acre southward extension in 1816 would be supervised by John Foster. The dock was originally built for the timber trade. The long hiatus in dock construction between Queens and Princes can be traced to the uncertainties of trade around the time of the French Revolutionary and Napoleonic Wars which gave   dock construction a low priority.   Like Kings, it was extensively altered at the start of the twentieth century to bring its century-old facilities up to date, with two branch docks to extend quay space and a graving dock for ship repair.   As in the rest of the South Docks, the facilities here were of insufficient use for the handling of modern ships and cargoes to justify the continued expense of dredging the channel and maintaining undersized and obsolescent quays and buildings. and the dock was closed to commercial shipping in 1972.

The dock was named after Queen Charlotte Sofia, the younger sister of Duke Adolphus Frederick IV, of Mecklenburg Strelitz and wife of George III (see Georges Dock.)   They married the day they met, 7 September 1761. Queen Charlotte has remained rather a background figure in history, though   she did her duty by bearing him fifteen children. Queen Charlotte had charge of his person and of the Royal Household during his bouts of insanity.

The new VAT offices straddle the former Queens Graving Dock.

Royal Seaforth Dock

Opened 1972

Still going strong: Liverpool's traditional timber trade, now at Royal Seaforth. (MD&HC)

The success story of the Mersey Docks was continued by the establishment of the Seaforth Dock. The consulting engineers were Rendel Palmer & Tritton, successors to J. M. Rendel, who fortunately did a much better job than his at the Great Low Water Basin! It would not be stretching the truth to say that the expansion here really saved the Port and arrested its decline. While modern cargo handling methods require far fewer employees than previously, the Seaforth Dock (backed up by modernisation of the adjoining older docks) has meant that Liverpool today handles as much cargo tonnage as in the supposed golden years at the end of last century. Seaforth handles containerised imports and exports to North and South America and Africa, including foods, wines and spirits, consumer goods, machine parts and so on. Terminals exist for bulk loads of cereals coming to the giant mills, the products of which go into bread and Kellogg's Cornflakes among other things. Bulk loads of copper, timber, newsprint and edible oils are also important. The establishment in 1984 of a Freeport where goods can be held for export without paying a variety of government taxes and duties, has greatly aided Seaforth's development. Compared to the rest of the docks, Seaforth does not have much of a history, but it is where the future of the Port of Liverpool lies.

The dock is 'Royal' because it was opened by Her Majesty the Queen and 'Seaforth', because of its geographical location. 'Seaforth' would seem to be of reasonably recent derivation, relating to its position for sea views.

The container berths at Seaforth. (MD&HC)

Salisbury Dock

Opened 1848

Salisbury/Trafalgar passage in 1980, when residences were still standing.

Salisbury Dock is the Half-Tide Dock serving as the entrance to the group opened in 1848. Its triple entrance (50ft and 60ft wide half-tide and 18ft boat lock) was briefly the largest and most convenient on the river, until the opening of Wellington Half-Tide in 1850. It also provided access to Clarence Graving Dock Basin, and thus had entrances or passages on all four sides: coupled with its small size of just under 3 1/2 acres, this meant it could only ever provide berths for quite small vessels. It remained greatly in demand by coastal vessels until the opening of the new coastal terminal at Waterloo Dock in 1971.

James Brownlow William Gascoyne Cecil was born in London on 17 April 1791. He served as Member of Parliament for Weymouth 1813-17 and thereafter for Hertford. His connection with Liverpool arose from his marrying a member of the famous old Liverpool family of Gascoyne, through which he acquired extensive property in West Derby. In 1823 he became second Marquis of Salisbury, whence the name of the Dock. He held a number of influential appointments, including Lord Lieutenant of Middlesex, Lord Privy Seal and Lord President of the Council, and died on 12 April 1868.

What is it about Salisbury entrance that makes photographers get all arty?

The Salthouse (South) Dock

Opened 1753 Extensive Alterations c.1850 Closed 1972

Salthouse seen from the roof of Albert Warehouses c. 1890.

Liverpool's second dock was constructed to the south of the first (Old) Dock on land reclaimed from the Mersey. Built entirely from stone, it was linked to the Old Dock and to the Mersey through a tidal basin. It was designed by Thomas Steers who died in 1750, and was succeeded as dock engineer by his clerk, Henry Berry. As with the Old Dock before it, the traffic was too great and too varied to allow it to develop any specialised trades. In the early part of its life it simply took whatever cargoes happened to be brought in by the ships crowding along its wharves, which was mainly agricultural produce from Ireland and the Mediterranean. As the docks expanded from their beginnings, the South Dock provided the basis for many connections. The construction of Albert, Canning and Wapping docks in the mid-nineteenth century and the filling of the Old Dock all went to alter the layout of the dock, which was by now called the Salthouse, so much that it had in effect been bodily moved. It settled into use as a loading berth for vessels which had discharged into the Albert warehouses, finally being closed to commercial traffic with the rest of the South Docks in 1972. The redevelopment of the derelict group around Albert has left the Salthouse Dock largely intact as recreational waterspace but without any of its dockside buildings, though a token of its unusual granite transit shed remains on the east side.

A recent view through the surviving gable end of one of the granite transit sheds.

The original name is obviously due to the dock's geographical location. The appellation of 'Salthouse' dates from around 1780 when further docks had been constructed and 'South Dock' was a growing source of confusion. Saltworks had existed on the site since the early eighteenth century, refining rock salt from Cheshire by dissolving it in water, then boiling the solution to cause fairly pure salt to recrystallise. The process, and hence the site, was notorious for the clouds of black smoke brought about, presumably, by the use of rather inferior coal. These works were owned by the Blackburnes of Warrington and lent their name to the dock.

Sandon Dock

Opened 1851   Altered 1901-2

The improved entrance to Sandon Half-Tide, c. 1903.

Accessed via a half-tide basin which also served Huskisson and Wellington Docks, Sandon was notable for no less than six graving docks that opened off from its north side, and the need for access to these sometimes hindered the use of the dock proper. The Sandon half-tide entrance was widened in 1892 to allow larger vessels to use it. In 1902, further improvements included a triple entrance which could be used as locks for small vessels but as half-tide gates for large ones, and the depth was increased to 6ft 6in deeper than at Canada Entrance, with the result that Sandon once again accommodated the giants of the North Atlantic. The graving docks had been largely superseded by the Herculaneum and Birkenhead facilities, and were lost in the construction of Huskisson Branch Dock One in 1902. The half-tide dock was remodelled and combined with the Wellington half-tide, to form a large new Sandon Half-Tide which gave turning space for very large ships. Today the site has passed into the hands of North West Water for a pumping station and sewage treatment works for the interceptor sewer scheme to clean up the waters of the Mersey.

Sandon Half-Tide with, to the left, the new sewage treatment works.

Lord Sandon was the courtesy title for the heir to the Earldom of Harrowby. The particular Lord Sandon after whom this dock was named was Dudley Ryder, born in the Army Pay Office, Whitehall, on 23 May 1798. He was educated at Christ Church, Oxford, where he was a friend of Francis Egerton, who also had a dock, albeit a highly inferior one, named after him. He graduated in 1820, by which time he was already serving as Member of Parliament for Tiverton. In 1831, he resigned as Member for Tiverton and was elected to represent Liverpool, and continued to serve until his father's death rendered him ineligible. He was, thus, MP for Liverpool at the time of the Act (1844) which enabled Sandon Dock. He occupied a number of important posts, including Chancellor of the Duchy of Lancaster and Lord Keeper of the Privy Seal, and he was also the President of the Society for the Prevention of Cruelty to Animals. He died on 19 November 1882.

Stanley Dock

Opened 1848   Closed 1988

The entrance to Stanley from Collingwood, with the Dock Road and the Overhead Railway in the background.

One of the more unusual of the Mersey Docks. The only dock on the landward side of the dock road and in some ways the biggest of all - running to Leeds! The direct access provided to the Leeds and Liverpool Canal via a flight of locks, was important in the carriage of bulky goods, especially coal downwards and imported cotton and wool upwards, and also in some distributive trades. It was also good business for the canal company who contributed £50,000 towards the link.   The original warehouses gave Stanley an appearance and mode of operation not unlike Albert and late last century it was heading for redundancy as surely as its predecessor. Stanley was kept in business by infilling about half its width and building a massive bonded tobacco warehouse erected in 1900, which dominates the dock, and indeed the area, to this day. It has 12 floors above quay level, with vaults below, and a floor area of 1.3 million square feet, and was capable of holding · 180,000 hogsheads of tobacco. It was consistently the most profitable of the Board's warehouses. Stanley Dock now has a number of temporary uses, but is effectively redundant and awaiting redevelopment.

The Sunday Market at Stanley, summer 1992.

Much of the history of Liverpool from the Norman Conquest to the reign of Victoria, involved the activities of the two great local landowning families, the Molyneuxs and the Stanleys. The Molyneuxs were the hereditary constables of Liverpool Castle, while the Stanleys had the control of the only other fortification in the town, the Tower. The Stanleys were Lords of Man and Earls of Derby. They played a prominent role in Liverpool, frequently representing the town as MP. The title of Lord Derby went to the male head of the family, while his heir was Lord Stanley as a courtesy title. The land required for the northwards extension of the docks was sold to the Liverpool Dock Trust by the thirteenth Earl of Derby in 1843 for £17,500. As a tribute to him and his family, one of the docks made on the land was named Stanley. It must also have helped that the Earl's son and grandson were both MPs. His son, by then the fourteenth Earl of Derby, would go on to have three terms as Prime Minister in 1852, 1858-59 and 1866-68.

Toxteth Dock

Opened 1841 Totally Rebuilt 1888 Closed 1972

Handling palm oil at Elder Dempster's appropriated berth, late 1920s.

Originally the name of a small tidal basin with the site enclosed by a wall. Described by Picton in 1875 as "the only spot in the long line of the Liverpool Docks where the grass grows on the quays", the small basin was largely by-passed by the trade of the Mersey. Like Harrington Dock (q.v.) the area around the basin was reserved for expansion when needed, and in 1888, the new, much larger Toxteth Dock, was opened. Harrington and Toxteth were the first docks in the port to be built with double storey transit sheds with rooftop cranes. When these proved to be successful, they spread to other Liverpool Docks. For many years Toxteth was home to the Harrison Line.

The dock is named after the district where it is built. Toxteth had a long history as a hunting park, formed originally by King John. It was not formally disafforested until the seventeenth century, and retained its rural character until the late eighteenth century. The name Toxteth would appear to be Norse in origin, derived from words meaning something like Toki's stead or the farm of Toki.

The two storey transit sheds after conversion.

Trafalgar Dock

Opened 1836, re-modelled 1929

The new Trafalgar Dock under construction.

Trafalgar Dock started life as a conventional rectangular basin with access from the river via either Victoria entrance to the South or Clarence Half-Tide to the North, and does not appear to have specialised in any particular trade. Like all its contemporaries, it soon suffered from overcrowding, necessitating more new docks to the north, and also from the growth of the size of ships, which soon rendered it obsolescent. It remained unmodernised until 1929, when Clarence was infilled and Clarence Graving Dock Basin, Clarence Half-Tide and the outer end of Trafalgar were formed into the present Trafalgar Dock, while the remainder of the old dock became Trafalgar Branch, which, together with most of Victoria, was infilled for the new coastal container terminal opened in 1971. These docks had rather a new lease of life with the opening of the new Waterloo Entrance in 1949. As it stands today, Trafalgar is totally unrecognisable as being related to its original form, having roughly doubled in length and turned through 90 degrees. It is still occasionally used by small warships visiting HMS Eaglet.

Trafalgar Dock 1992, looking North.

The dock is named after the Battle of Trafalgar which ensured British naval supremacy in the Napoleonic Wars, removing the threat of invasion and adding to the myth of British naval invincibility. A fleet of 33 French and Spanish ships under the French Admiral, Pierre Villeneuve, were intercepted by 27 British ships of the line under Nelson. Villeneuve was under pressure to move to support French forces in Italy under Marshal Massena, and Napoleon had threatened to remove him from his position for cowardice. Nelson had been pursuing Villeneuve for six months. Despite the Franco-Spanish fleet's numerical superiority when the two columns of

British ships attacked the allied line at right angles, eighteen of the French fleet were captured and only eleven reached Cadiz. No British ships were lost. To quote Dupuy: "Nelson had destroyed French naval power and established Britain as the mistress of the seas in the most decisive major naval victory - tactically and strategically - of history". Little wonder that the Dock Trustees wished to celebrate this victory in the naming of the dock and to emphasise the power of the Royal Navy to visiting foreigners.

Union Dock

Opened 1889

The site of the second Union Dock, which dissappeared during construction of the New Brunswick Entrance (right).

A very small basin of less than one acre formed in 1889 to link the new Toxteth Dock with the Brunswick Dock and so enable easy movement of ships along the South Docks without the need to enter the river. It was very short lived, disappearing in the major South Docks improvements at the start of this century. This was the second Union Dock in Liverpool (for the first, see Coburg Dock).On one level the names of both docks are simply related to their function in 'uniting' two groups of docks. There is also, however, the possibility that these docks were named as political statements related to the 'union' of Britain with Ireland, which was a current issue at the time of the naming of both Union Docks (1816 and 1889), though it was admittedly so for much of the nineteenth century.

Victoria Dock

Opened 1834   Closed 1988

Coast Lines' Terrier in Trafalgar, bound for Victoria, which is just out of picture to the right. The nearest we could get to a picture of Victoria in traffic.

A very similar dock to Trafalgar, which opened on the same day, Victoria was originally built with its own entrance from the river, but this was closed in 1846, leaving Victoria, Trafalgar and Waterloo as the first real examples of spine and branch docks, though the expression was not yet in use. Like Trafalgar and Clarence, it languished unmodernised until 1929. Waterloo, Trafalgar and Victoria docks formed the last group to be opened specifically for sail. Every dock that followed would make at least minor concessions towards the growth of steam.

Named for Princess Victoria when she was the heir apparent to William IV. When Princess Charlotte, daughter of George IV, died in childbirth in 1817, the lack of a close heir to the throne prompted all of George's brothers to marry. Victoria was born on 24 May 1819, the daughter of the Duke and Duchess of Kent. In 1825 she was recognised as the likely successor to William IV, as neither of his legitimate children survived infancy. Victoria acceded to the throne on 20 June, 1837. Her predecessors were unkindly if not unfairly, described by Sir Sidney Lee as "an imbecile, a profligate and a buffoon" (George III, George IV and William IV respectively), so the coronation of a pretty young woman after three eccentric and unappealing Kings was greeted with popular enthusiasm. Victoria became a close friend of Lord Melbourne, the Prime Minister. She had first met Albert (see Albert Dock) in 1836 with her Uncle Leopold, King of the Belgians acting as matchmaker. The two were married on 10 February, 1840. The first of their children, Victoria, was born in November of that year. Over the next 17 years Victoria had a further eight children. In their private life the Royal Family were almost a typical Victorian middle-class family.

The sad remains of the costal container terminal stand on the infilled Victoria Dock.

The death of Albert on 14 December, 1861, left the Queen devastated. For much of the next twenty years the Queen remained almost a recluse in mourning for her husband. During this time her popularity fell - it was proposed that the Queen should abdicate in favour of the Prince of Wales, and several attempts were made on her life. In May 1876 she was declared Empress of India. The recovery of the Prince of Wales from a life threatening bout of typhoid and her growing public appearances through the 1880s led to a surge in her personal popularity, and the jubilee celebrations for her fiftieth and sixtieth years on the throne were immense and happy affairs. Her death on 22 January, 1901 really did mark the end of an era. Her family married into the royal families of Norway, Sweden, Russia, Spain, Germany and Greece, as well as becoming related to a host of lesser nobles. A large proportion of the nobility of Western Europe today are in some way related to Victoria.

Vittoria Dock

Commenced 1905 Completed 1909 Extended 1951

Vittoria under construction, 1907.

Originally this area was land reclaimed by the dock construction from the Wallasey Pool. When walled, it became known as Vittoria Wharf, a large open area used for timber storage, railway marshalling and the erection of temporary sheds. The quays were used in the general trade, with coal tips and Rea's jetty located at the western end. Growing dissatisfaction was voiced by the Far Eastern traders with the facilities at the shallow and undersized Morpeth and Egerton docks. The increasing size of their ships led to continued pressure for new accommodation which was eventually provided by the construction of the Vittoria Dock. A large basin constructed off the East Float, the new Dock was actually slightly smaller in area than the Morpeth and Egerton Docks it largely superseded but much more conveniently shaped for access than the narrow triangles and parallelograms of the older pair. Shipping companies, including such famous names as Brocklebank's, Holt and Clan lines relocated here. The dock was extended to the west in the fifties to provide better berths as the ships continued to increase in size. With the decline of breakbulk traffic, Vittoria seemed to have little future, but a revival recently has led to ambitious plans for new investment.

There is now a considerable revival of traffic, where once decline seemed irreversible.

The Battle of Vittoria was fought on 21 June 1813, and was the decisive battle of the Peninsular War in Spain. It marked the expulsion of the main French force from the Iberian Peninsula and hence the beginning of rolling back Napoleon's conquests as a prelude to his eventual defeat. The Duke of Wellington leading 80,000 troops defeated King Joseph Bonaparte and 65,000 men. There are a few sources that suggest that this wharf was initially known as 'Victoria'. This leads to two options, either they are misprints or the name was changed when the Birkenhead docks were acquired by the Liverpool Corporation to avoid confusion with the Victoria dock on the other side of the Mersey. Certainly the original plans for the Birkenhead scheme of 1843 included a Victoria Dock on this site.

Wallasey Dock

Commenced 1874 Completed 1877

Four masted barque Garthpool *in Wallasey Dock.*

This dock was converted from the Low Water Basin (q.v.) by building a wall across the entrance. Extensive quantities of silt were removed by dredgers and thousands of piles were driven in to the soft bottom of the basin to provide a strong foundation for the new construction, using concrete blocks to wall off the basin. The landing stages of the Low Water Basin were removed and the indentations in the walls of the basin which they left were filled with staging. Warehouses and transit sheds were erected around the dock. The ill-advised nature of the Low Water Basin was further illustrated by the difficulties in the Wallasey Dock/East Float entrance passage. Designed originally as the main entrance to the entire Birkenhead system, it was quickly found to be too small and Wallasey dock went rapidly downhill in terms of shipping usage. Initially the sheds were mainly used for grain storage but they soon became enveloped in the Foreign Animals Wharf for imported cattle, sheep and pigs. The 'curse' of the Low Water Basin quickly reared its head again when the Wallasey

Dock began to silt up once more at the turn of the century. In 1890 a pumping station was erected on the river wall to move river water into the Birkenhead Docks to increase their effective depth. This water carried silt which was deposited in the dock and slowly began to fill it up. This more or less finished off the dock and by the 1960s it was useless, the sheds becoming industrial units. Today the dock stands derelict, awaiting redevelopment.

The name is directly derived from Wallasey Pool, as the dock is built on reclaimed land in what was once the mouth of that tidal inlet. There was a proposal to name it the 'America Dock', in the same manner as the Canada, a tribute to a major trading partner but 'Wallasey' was felt to be more appropriate. Wallasey itself is derived from Old English meaning the island of the Welshmen or strangers. Prior to the dock construction, Wallasey was indeed almost an island cut off by Wallasey Pool and marshland from the rest of the Wirral.

Redevelopment at Wallasey Docks has begun, but the impounding station at the far end will remain.

Wapping Dock

Opened 1855 Altered 1905 Closed 1972

Wapping Warehouses between the wars, and past their best.

Built as part of Jesse Hartley's programme to rationalise the South Docks to keep pace with the new group of 1848-52 docks from Salisbury to Huskisson in the North. Like the Coburg alteration, Wapping was constructed principally to improve communication between existing docks. The presence of the privately owned Dukes Dock had resulted in Salthouse and Kings Docks having no connection. That meant that if a vessel needed to move from one dock to another, it had to lock out into the river and back in again, a time-consuming and wasteful process. A linking passage would solve this problem, provide much-needed extra quay space and reduce the use of entrances. It would also lower the number of entrances required and as they are the most expensive element of a dock to construct, maintain and operate, this was a most desirable result.

The East Quay has a warehouse of similar design to those at Albert. Part of the Wapping Railway Goods Station was absorbed by the building of this dock, and the warehouse had a railway line running inside it. This was removed in 1878 as it had received little use over the preceding twenty years, and indicates the difficulties the Liverpool Docks had in coming to terms with railways. Wapping's main use was always as a passage dock, though the warehouse did see a wide variety of cargoes. The dock was altered in connection with the Kings/Queens alteration at the beginning of this century. The warehouse today has been successfully converted into flats.

This portion of what is generally called the "Dock Road" is officially named Wapping, and although it has been altered, re- aligned and widened several times, the name itself goes back at least to the late eighteenth century. The district for a few hundred yards radius from the railway goods terminus was also known as Wapping. The name does not have any long-standing local connection, and is, like those of Whitechapel or Soho Street, a borrowing of an old London district name.

Waterloo Dock

Opened 1834   Extensively Altered c.1868   Closed 1988

Waterloo Corn Warehouses in 1877.

Originally much like its neighbours Victoria and Trafalgar, Waterloo was eventually altered beyond recognition. In 1844 an observatory was erected on the dock wall to provide accurate time-checks for ships' chronometers, which were essential for safe navigation.   This observatory moved to Bidston Hill on the Wirral in 1867, where it continued to provide important and inventive solutions to navigation problems. The reason for the move, aside from pollution problems making observation difficult, was a massive redevelopment plan for the Dock. The growth in the trade in cereal crops after the repeal of the Corn Laws, saw an increasing demand for storage space on the Dock Estate. Waterloo Dock was divided in two by a quay built north-south, forming two smaller docks, East and West Waterloo. East Waterloo became home to massive grain warehouses with the latest equipment for handling and storing grain in bulk.   After some early teething troubles, the warehouses proved reasonably successful, but rapid progress in handling machinery soon made them obsolescent. Part of one block was turned into a mill in 1904, and in 1925 they were completely re-equipped for handling oil seeds. West Waterloo continued as a passage dock between Victoria and Princes half- tide, with some berth space on its long sides. An entrance lock into West Waterloo was proposed just prior to World War II, finally being completed in 1949. Today, the Waterloo Dock is subject to the same re-development proposals as the Princes Dock and the remaining grain warehouse block, G.F. Lyster's architectural triumph, is being converted into flats.

The warehouses during conversion into flats.

Named for the battle that spelled the end of Napoleon's wars in Europe. Napoleon Bonaparte had abdicated in April 1814, but returned from exile on Elba to mainland France on 1 March 1815. France was faced by the armies of all the major European powers. Napoleon's plan was to defeat each of his opponents in turn, beginning with the British, Prussian and Dutch armies in Belgium, before his other main opponents the Austrians and Russians could mobilise to interfere. After a period of manoeuvre, the campaign reached its climax at the Battle of Waterloo in Belgium. A French Army of 72,000 under Napoleon clashed with 68,000 mainly British and Dutch troops under Wellington on 18 June 1815. By 4 o'clock the allied forces had been pushed back at all points. Wellington's counter attack and the arrival of Blucher with 61,000 Prussians shattered French resistance. The Prussians had been defeated two days previously at Ligny by a French army led by Marshal Grouchy, but Grouchy had failed to press home his advantage, leaving Blucher able to tip the scales in what proved to be the decisive battle. Napoleon abdicated his position as Emperor of France on 21 June 1815, and was exiled to St. Helena where he died on 5 May 1821.

Wellington Dock

Opened 1850

Wellington in the early years of the century; past its prime, but still busy.

Another of the docks under the 1844 Act, Wellington was originally entered via its own half-tide dock. Like Nelson and Bramley-Moore, it had a temporary "flagship" role while the larger docks to the North were still under construction. In 1856 the High Level Coal Railway (see Bramley Moore Dock) occupied its East quay. The works of 1901-2 (see Sandon Dock) made access much easier, and Wellington became a centre for trades with Northern Europe. When the High Level Railway closed, its structure was partly demolished so as to form storage cells for gravel, a trade which still continues there.

Arthur Wellesley, first Duke of Wellington, 'the Iron Duke', is widely regarded as the greatest general Britain has ever produced. Born in 1759, the fourth son of the Irish peer, Lord Mornington, he was educated at Eton and (somewhat ironically) at a French military school at Angers. His military career was characterised by rapid promotion. At the age of twenty four he was the Lieutenant Colonel commanding the 33rd Regiment, and was already a member of the Irish Parliament. In 1798 his brother Lord Mornington, was appointed Governor General of Bengal, India, and the 33rd were ordered there. In 1802 Wellesley was a Major General in the Indian Army. In 1805 he returned to England and was elected to the Westminster Parliament. In 1807-8 he served as Irish Chief Secretary. Between 1809 and 1815 he master-minded the British campaigns against the French, leading to the final victory at Waterloo, and his creation as Duke of Wellington. In 1818 he was appointed Master General of the Ordnance. In 1827 he was Commander-in-Chief of the British Armed Forces, and in 1828 he was Prime Minister. After a career as long as it was distinguished, he died on 14 September 1852.

The sand and gravel trade at Wellington.

The Woodside Basin

Opened 1847 ˙ Closed 1870

The imposing entrance to the Docks at Shore Road. Woodside Basin would have been in the background had the photographer got there 122 years earlier.

Constructed as part of the Birkenhead Dock development. The original purpose of this three-sided tidal basin was to provide a shelter and home for the small craft that were displaced from the Wallasey Pool by the docks being built there. (Such provisions were quite common as a means of buying off opposition to a Parliamentary Bill, as in the case of the Liverpool South Ferry Basin) A gridiron was provided: this was a sturdy iron frame over which a boat could be floated at high water. Low water left it perched on the frame, allowing a couple of hours during which minor repairs, such as a bit of caulking, could be effected. There was also a ferry landing pier for the Woodside to Liverpool service. The construction of the Morpeth Branch Dock involved the closure of the basin and the building of a river wall along the open side. Such extensive remodelling of the rest of the basin was carried out as to leave nothing recognisable of its previous form.

The basin's name comes from the ferry at Woodside Point, which faced Seacombe across the widest point of the mouth of Wallasey Pool. Birkenhead derives its name from a forest - the name developing from Old Norse words for a headland covered with birches. 'Woodside' came into use because the ferry point was beside a wood.

Other Docks on the Mersey.

By no means all of the docks on the river are part of the Port of Liverpool, and some of them have commemorative names, rather after the style of Liverpool Docks, which sometimes cause confusion. There follows a short list of these other docks, in geographical order, moving upstream.

<u>Princess Dock</u>
Often confused with Princes Dock, Princess Dock is the very large graving dock belonging to Cammell Laird, close to the Birkenhead Priory.
<u>Bromborough Dock</u> and <u>Port Sunlight Dock</u>
Both these were built to serve the vegetable oil based industries which grew up around the original Lever soap works. Bromborough Dock was much the larger and more modern of the two and survived until 1987.

New Dock, Garston.

<u>Old Dock (Garston), New Dock,</u> and <u>Stalbridge Dock.</u>
Garston Docks were started by the St Helens and Runcorn Gap Railway

Company in 1846, but were taken over by the London & North Western Railway, who invested heavily in them as a competitor to Liverpool. Initially they were heavily geared to coal export, but increasingly moved into other trades. Garston is now a highly successful little port, with a good trade in containers, imported steel and exported scrap. Ironically, when Liverpool is importing vast amounts of low-sulphur coal for electricity generation, Garston still *exports* coal.

Queen Elizabeth II Dock.

By the end of World War 2, it was becoming clear that the largest tankers would soon reach a size which would prevent them reaching Stanlow Docks. (see below) The Port of Manchester therefore took the bold decision to construct a large new dock adjacent to the Ship Canal entrance at Eastham. Opened in 1954, it was soon obsolete for "supertankers", but remains very adequate for what are now medium sized vessels, especially those from Central and South American ports.

Stanlow Docks

Manchester was not content that Liverpool should monopolise the rapidly growing oil importing trade, and constructed two docks in a rock "island" on the offshore side of the Ship Canal at Stanlow. Number 1 opened in 1916 and Number 2 in 1933. They are still in use.

Delamere Dock and Tollemache Dock

The Trustees of the Weaver Navigation were originally rather unimaginative, using names as lyrical as "The Basin". When titles like "The even newer basin" beckoned, they named the biggest of their docks at Weston Point in 1870 and 1885 after local landowners. Weston Point Docks have a troubled recent history, but are open again at the time of writing.

Fenton Dock, Runcorn.

<u>Francis Dock, Alfred Dock, Arnold Dock</u> and <u>Fenton Dock.</u>
The Bridgewater Trustees also resisted the use of names for a long time, but increasing complication of their system brought about surrender in 1850. The other named docks followed in 1860, 1870 and 1875 respectively. Alfred and Fenton Docks are still in use.

The zenith of the dock builders art; West Bank Dock Widnes.

<u>Widnes Dock</u> and <u>West Bank Dock</u>

Widnes Dock is now part of the Spike Island park, but was the first purpose-built railway dock in the world. It did not have a distinguished history, and was soon supplanted by Garston, which had access to much deeper water. West Bank Dock did not suffer so much from lack of water, as it was mainly intended for use by flats anyway. It was a small creek with the edges tidied up (a bit) and gates at its mouth. Undoubtedly the tattiest effort on the Mersey to be dignified with the name of "Dock".

<u>Anonymous.</u>

If Stanlow Docks only just qualify as having names, Ellesmere Port Docks, which were quite an extensive system, fall the other side of the divide in resolutely refusing to have names or even numbers. Instead, they used

113

simple descriptive titles like "The Raddle Wharf" or "The Mill Arm", which probably served just as well for organising berths.

Minor Basins.

Liverpool had a number of very small tidal basins in addition to those mentioned above, of which only one survives, namely South Ferry Basin which was completed about 1820, just to the north of what became Coburg Dockyard. Provided with a slipway, its customers deserted it in favour of the floating stage, and it became the home of the shrinking Liverpool fishing fleet, hence its colloquial name of "The Cockle 'Ole". Liverpool Corporation kept up two small ferry basins, Georges Ferry Basin and Seacombe Ferry Basin, the latter surviving until the extension of the floating stage, completed in 1876. They also had the River Craft Dock, and Eagle Basin (just south of Dukes) which totalled just over 1.5 acres and had sills *above* Old Dock Sill. Further south, Anderton Basin, which disappeared in the New South Works, was of 1198 square yards. In at least one case, Billingsgate Basin, partly completed new works (at Waterloo) were temporarily worked as a tidal basin for construction materials and for undemanding traffics such as landing fish.

GLOSSARY

Basin : An area of water partially enclosed from the river for ease of unloading small vessels, to provide calm water for manoeuvring into an enclosed dock, and as a refuge from foul weather. Tidal basins were usually rectangular, but some strange shapes also appeared, as at Canada.

Birkenhead Docks : The docks on the Cheshire side of the river begun by private builders and taken over by the MD&HB. Despite being called 'Birkenhead' Docks, around half of them are actually in Wallasey.

Spine and Branch : Later Mersey Docks are built with a spine linked to entrances or other docks and branches - dead ends lined with berth facilities. A 'spine and branch' dock offers more quay length in the same area than a traditional dock.

Central Docks : Those Liverpool Docks from George's Dock (now the Pier Head) northwards to Bramley Moore; are now mostly disused and awaiting re-development under M.D.C. auspices.

Dry Dock : Archaic name for a tidal basin (i.e. one which dried out at low tide). Not to be confused with a graving dock.

Dock : Generally applied to any enclosed area of water for loading, discharging, laying up or repairing ships or, more specifically, an enclosed excavated "hole" which retains water within it to allow ships to float, unless it is deliberately emptied.

Dock, graving : A dock which can have the water run or pumped from it to allow a vessel to sit on blocks for repair purposes. When the repairs are completed, water can be re-admitted to allow the ship to leave. Also, more recently and rather confusingly, called a dry dock. "Graving" means scratching: a graving dock was where you went to scratch off rust, barnacles and the like from your ship's bottom.

Dock, wet   : A dock which retains sufficient water for a ship to remain afloat at all times. (or to sink in if there is something seriously wrong!)

**Half-tide Basin
or Dock**   : A basin (q.v.) with an access to tidal water closed by a single pair of gates. These gates are opened or closed when the tide is about half way in or out, whence the name half-tide. When the tide is coming in, the gates are opened when the level outside is roughly equal to that inside, allowing vessels to move in and out. When the tide has ebbed about half way, the gates are closed, holding sufficient water within to keep at least the smaller vessels afloat in the basin.

Impounding   : Holding water above its natural level. All wet docks impound water between high tides - that is what they are for. Some docks had, and the Birkenhead system still has, artificial impounding (by huge pumps) to gain depth at neap tides.

Lock   : Like a lock on a canal - a rectangular passage with gates at either end. Water can be run in or out to allow vessels to move from one level to another. On the Mersey their use was particularly advantageous (as compared with tidal or half-tide entrances) because they minimised the loss of impounded water - which also minimised the influx of silt-bearing tidal water to restore the level. They also provided much more freedom for smaller ships to enter and leave at various states of the tide.

North Docks : Originally, The Liverpool Docks north of the Pier Head, now used to mean those north of Bramley Moore and still operational under MD&HC control.

Pier Head. : Originally used to mean the "nose" of any river entrance, later came to imply the George's Pier Head. (Just South of the Stokers' Monument, St Nicholas Place) Now used more loosely to cover the area bounded by the river, James Street, the Dock Road and St Nicholas Place.

South Docks : The Liverpool Docks South of Pier Head, closed to shipping in 1972, now re-developed for commercial, residential and recreational purposes.

Spine Dock : See Spine and Branch.

Give a Dock A Good Name?
Bibliography

Dictionary of National Biography, London, 1897 (and additional volumes).

J.M. Dodgson, Place Names of Cheshire (Part IV), Cambrige, 1972.

R.E. & T.N. Dupuy, Encyclopaedia of Military History 3500 BC to present - 2nd Edition, London, 1986.

J. Keegan & A. Wheatcroft, Who's Who In Military History, London, 1976.

The Mersey Docks and Harbour Board Collection, Maritime Records Centre, Merseyside Maritime Museum.

Further Reading

This work gives a necessarily brief overview of the history of the Port. More detailed information can be found in the following:

General History:

F.E. Hyde, <u>Liverpool and the Mersey</u>, Newton Abbot, 1971 - Strong on economic history, but getting a little dated now.

S. Mountfield, <u>Western Gateway</u>, Liverpool, 1965 - Written by the former secretary to the Dock Board, drawing on MD&HB archives, it has the advantages and the drawbacks of an insider's view.

A.E. Jarvis, <u>Docks of the Mersey</u>, Shepperton, 1988 - Broad overview of all the Port facilities of the river

Specific Docks

N. Ritchie-Noakes, <u>Liverpool's Historic Waterfront</u>, London, 1984 - Detailed work on Liverpool's South Docks

A. Jarvis, <u>Liverpool Central Docks 1799-1905</u>, Stroud, 1991 - Concentrating on engineering and political developments in the Central Docks' history.

A. Jarvis. <u>Princes Dock</u>, Merseyside Port Folios, 1991.

K. McCarron. <u>Meat at Woodside: The Birkenhead Livestock Trade 1878-1981</u>, Merseyside Port Folios, 1991.

K. McCarron, <u>The Fall and Rise of Birkenhead Docks</u>, Merseyside Port Folios, forthcoming. The early history of the Birkenhead group of Docks

119